TURTLE ISLAND ALPHABET

• • •

For Victor —
in appreciation
for "Tesuqve poems" —
Salute across the
arroyo.

in friendship,
Gerry Hausman

Tesuqve (other side)
Summer '94

TURTLE ISLAND ALPHABET

ALPHABET

• • •

A LEXICON OF NATIVE AMERICAN SYMBOLS AND CULTURE

GERALD HAUSMAN

ST MARTIN'S PRESS
NEW YORK

TURTLE ISLAND ALPHABET: A Lexicon of Native American Symbols and Culture. Copyright © 1992 by Gerald Hausman. All rights reserved. Printed in the United States of America. No part of this book may be used or reproduced in any manner whatsoever without written permission except in the case of brief quotations embodied in critical articles or reviews. For information, address St. Martin's Press, 175 Fifth Avenue, New York, N.Y. 10010.

Library of Congress Cataloging-in-Publication Data
Hausman, Gerald
    Turtle Island alphabet : a lexicon of Native American symbols and culture / Gerald Hausman : introduction by N. Scott Momaday.
        p.   cm.
      ISBN 0-312-07103-5 (hc)
      ISBN 0-312-09406-X (pbk.)
      1. Indians of North America—Religion and mythology.   2. Indians of North America—Dictionaries.   3. Indians of North America—Legends. I. Title.
E98.R3H27   1992
398.2′08997DC20   91-36523   CIP

"Mountain Lion" from *The Complete Poems of D.H. Lawrence* by D.H. Lawrence, Eds. de Sola Pinto & Roberts. Copyright © 1964, 1971, by Angelo Ravagli and C.M. Weekly, Executors of the Estate of Freida Lawrence Ravagli. Used by permission of Viking Penguin, a division of Penguin Books USA, Inc.

"Big Shell Man," and "The Great Kiva" from *The Great Kiva: A Poetic Critique of Religion* by Phillips Kloss; "Rainbow Obsidian" from *Rainbow Obsidian* by Phillips Kloss. Both books courtesy of The Sunstone Press, Santa Fe.

Selections of Robert Boissiere from *Po Pai Mo: The Search for White Buffalo Woman* by Robert Boissiere; The Sunstone Press, P.O. Box 2321, Santa Fe, NM 87504-2321.

Quotation from Frank Waters ℗ *Masked Gods: Navajo and Pueblo Ceremonialism.* Published by Ohio University Press/Swallow Press.

The Sunstone notecards appearing in this book are from full-color notecards available from The Sunstone Press, P.O. Box 2321, Santa Fe, NM 87504-2321.

Cover Credits: All images are credited in the text except "Cayman Monotype" and "Feathered Serpent Monotype" by Ross Lew Allen. "Wolf Warrior" by Kevin Martin is reproduced courtesy of The Institute of American Indian Arts Museum, P.O. Box 20007, Santa Fe, NM 87504.

Design by Janet Tingey

First Paperback Edition: May 1993

10 9 8 7 6 5 4 3 2 1

CONTENTS

◆ ◆ ◆

ACKNOWLEDGMENTS

◆ ◆ ◆

I wish to thank the following individuals and organizations who helped in the preparation of this book: Will Channing, Sacred Circle; the librarians of the Santa Fe Public Library; Steve Rogers and Unis Kahn, Wheelright Museum of the American Indian; Chuck Dailey, Institute of American Indian Art; Michael Gleeson, Blue Harbour, Jamaica; Swallow Press/Ohio University Press; University of New Mexico Press; Gloria Levitas, Queens College; the Bureau of American Ethnology; Gerry and Barbara Clow, Bear and Company; Jim Smith, Sunstone Press; Willow Powers, Laboratory of Anthropology; Bob and Mary Ann Kapoun, the Rainbow Man; Ross LewAllen, Ross LewAllen Jewelry; Larry Feinstein, Lotus Audio Ltd.; Bobbe Besold, photographer; Visions Photo; Lightworks of Santa Fe; Joe Hedrick, photographer; Kitty King, archive researcher.

The following writers were invaluable to me. Without them, this book would not have come about: Roger Zelazny, Jay de Groat, Loren Straight Eagle Plume, Larry Littlebird, Harold Littlebird, Paul Metcalf, Frank Waters, Joseph Bruchac, Jr., David Kherdian, Jan Wiener, Sid Hausman, Phillips Kloss, Charles Lovato, Robert Boissiere.

Special thanks to my agent, Ricia Mainhardt, my editor, Robert Weil, and assistant editor Richard Romano, and my format-editor, Laura Ware.

And those more patient than patience, my family: Lorry, Mariah, and Hannah.

FOREWORD

◆ ◆ ◆

Arrow, bear, camp, doll. We who look into this book are literate human beings, and we are obliged to love alphabets. The alphabet is arguably the greatest of our inventions, nearly so great as to exceed our capacity for belief. If I remember his fine story rightly, Jorge Luis Borges defines the *aleph*, the first letter of the Hebrew alphabet, as the point in space in which all other points in space are contained. If a single letter can signify so much—the infinite, by and large—how potent then are words, lines, stories? We are confronting the miracle of language.

Gerald Hausman constructs an alphabet in alphabetic language. Another aspect of the miracle of language is the irony of this construction, for the objects of this alphabet are located in oral tradition. The Native Americans of that tradition, whose catalogue of basics this is, had an acute knowledge of arrows, bears, camps, and dolls, but they had no alphabet.

We are given "pieces of shell, bits of memory," but we are given much more than that. We are given the best possessions of a culture, its stuff of story, its sacred matter, its elemental and most cherished belongings.

It is implicit in these pages that the keepers of oral tradition had a deeper belief in language than have most of us in general. Language was the repository of their well-being, their past and their posterity, the irresistible current of their daily lives. In it their very being was defined and confirmed. And it lay on the plane of the human voice. It was always but one generation from extinction. Words were necessarily spoken *carefully,* they were listened to *carefully,* and they were remembered *carefully.* The alternative was irretrievable loss. The lore of this book is a true reflection of that concern. It is a lore that enriches and ennobles us. And we ought to hold it to our minds and hearts with all our strength.

My grandmother performed the intricate, minute motions of beadwork into her eighties. Her moccasins, which I have now in my possession, are exquisite to the eye and to the touch. They are, as Gerald Hausman says of moccasins, practical, lovely, and simple. I have worn my own moccasins, which are beaded in the design of the buffalo hoof, in the Kiowa Gourd Dance for many years. I have never worn shoes more serviceable or comfortable. In the dance I have the sense that I am barefoot, that the skin which touches the earth is mine. My moccasins and I and the earth are of one sacred reality.

The moccasin (the bead, the basket, the shield) is a thing that brings many disparate and holy elements together: earth, wind, words, music, the eternal masks of ceremony. The principal value of this alphabet is that it reminds us of the deepest meanings, the most common denominators, the very vitals of our human being. We look into this lexicon of the Native American, as into the whorls of a winter count, and we see the universe.

N. Scott Momaday
Tucson, 1991

INTRODUCTION
CARRYING WATER IN THE DESERT

◆ ◆ ◆

. . . we are all one, indivisible. Nothing that any of us does but affects us all.
—*From THE MAN WHO KILLED THE DEER* BY FRANK WATERS

Once, while I was giving a talk at a gathering in Florida, an edu-
cated white liberal raised his hand and asked, "What place do *we*
have in the native tradition of this country—we who have done
our best to destroy the old ways?" The answer that I gave him
came from a Santee Sioux medicine man with whom I had recently done a program in New York. He had been asked that question,
and I remembered his reply. "The time has come," he said, "to
bury our dead horses."

But what of the myths, which some say belong to the human
race? Who is responsible for them? Where do we, in the culture at
large, place ourselves here? Are we mute listeners, who, having lost
our way, must now rely on the wiser words and footsteps of those
whom we tried to extinguish? The answer to these questions came
to me from my friend, the Pueblo writer and storyteller, Larry
Littlebird. "God is incredibly generous," he said. "How am I not to
be like that? What am I supposed to do, hold on to it all?"

Another Native American spokesperson commented that it is
the moral truth in the myths that gives them life, currency, meaning. With television conquering more minds than do books, she

*Zuni Water Carriers Descending
from Thunder Mountain.* Acrylic.
Kristi Davis. Courtesy Sunstone
Press.

believed that storytelling carried the seeds of the future. We must trust in one another to tell the truths that have always been told, with our unpremeditated tongues, not with scripts that have been written for us.

As a mythologist who has spent much of his adult life recording Native American stories, I believe that we are all purveyors of wisdom, from whatever culture we may come . How we interpret what we hear is the only thing that separates one truth from another in other words, literally, how well we hear. Often enough, I return to my own mythic beginnings: a father who had Hungarian gypsy blood, a mother with Iroquois ancestry. At an early age, I was taught by my grandfather to treasure the word *myth*. When I was eight and he was more than eighty, he said to me, "Touch my hand." I did what he asked. Then he added, "You have now touched the hand that touched the hand that touched the hand of George Washington."

Momentarily stunned, I asked how such a thing was possible. "Simple," he said. "When I was your age, I met a woman who as a girl had been asked to dance with George Washington at his inaugural ball." My father joined in with the fact that when he was eight, he went to Buffalo Bill's Wild West Show and actually shook the old rounder's hand. Somehow the centuries came together when my family met and talked, swapping stories. My father, meeting Buffalo Bill, passed on to me the legend of a soft buckskin glove.

My grandfather's hand in history, so to speak, made the country seem small, time foreshortened, made me as a boy feel both young and old. Once, around the same time, my mother took my brother and me to meet a Cheyenne elder named Grey Wolf, who had seen the last of the great buffalo herds. His voice, when I first heard it, had the grease of bear, the song of sage in it. And it seemed to me, growing up, that I was forever seeing into the eyes of people who had done many things that were lost to the rest of the world. I

wondered, even as a child, if this would also be true of me. Would I see and hear things that, one day, would fit only the shape of words?

From my grandfather, I learned that one does not need to travel far to find legends. One of his ancestors from the eighteenth century had been eaten by a wolf pack, or so the tale was told. In any case, when the Berkshire snows melted, they found the squire's bones gnawed through the marrow, and thus the legend sprang forth, much to our delight. My great-aunt lost her husband to a gunman who shot him through the door of his riverside saloon. One country swain went to the goldfields of California via the Isthmus of Panama, and my brother, when he turned twenty, was damned if he didn't follow in his footsteps. Our mother, in 1932, climbed into a rumble-seated roadster and drove with her best girlfriend across country to see the last rivers of wild horses and visit with the Navajo. She camped with a sheepherder named Grizzly Rat, ate mutton and blackberries in his prairie schooner hidden in the tall grass of starry Wyoming.

So, I grew up living in a kettle of legends, which, at any moment, seemed ready to boil over. Often memory and myth overlapped to such a degree that it was impossible to separate the strands of the silky web woven by the family storytellers, who never lied and also probably never told the exact truth. As a boy, I gathered these myths and wrote them down, having accepted early on that I was the inheritor of them. In college, in northern New Mexico, it became clear, at least to me, that I would try somehow to make my hobby into a manageable living. I started by recording Navajo legends told to me by my roommate, Jay de Groat, whose Navajo name was Bluejay. "Be patient," he used to tell me, "our stories cannot be told out of season." If it was spring, I would wait until winter. However, one story that Jay began in the fall of 1965, he just recently finished telling one week ago—twenty-five years after he had started it.

Jay's grandfather was not a history gatherer like mine; he was a history maker. During the final years of the Apache resistance in the Southwest, Jay's grandfather tracked Geronimo. So I began with Jay's family, branched off into other Navajo families, and, for some time after college, delved into the Armenian family of writer David Kherdian. What struck me with the Armenian myths was that, aside from certain cultural differences, they were very similar to those of the Navajo. In fact, I learned that it was their differences, culturally speaking, that made them the same. And always, hidden within the tale, was the secreted diamond of every family: how, by hook or by crook, they contrived not to die. How, as a family of rough-cut tailors, determined not to lose their cloth, they wove themselves into the world, and so lived to see the day.

From the pogroms suffered by the Navajo, to the pogroms suffered by the Armenians, to the pogroms suffered by my father's family in Hungary—it was all, essentially, the same. It was one suffering. I added to these the stories of the Holocaust told to me by the Czech writer Jan Wiener, and saw that his matched Jay's, which matched David's, which matched my father's. I began, then, to compare. If this was the sorrow, where was the triumph? In the words of Jay de Groat, from his family's story of The Long Walk, in the book *Whimpering Chant:*

knowing
 he has endured
   his whimper turned into a chant
   far off over his homeland
 a loud rumble
   announced his return

 i see on the holy wind
 my brothers in all four directions
   for they too
   wept the Whimpering Chant

Ká yati-Sia (Zia). Photograph by Edward S. Curtis. Courtesy Rainbow Man, Santa Fe.

And in the words of David Kherdian, writing of his mother's mythic Armenian travail, in the book *The Road from Home:*

For as long as I knew the sky and clouds, we lived in our white stucco house in the Armenian quarter of Azizya, in Turkey, but when the great dome of Heaven cracked and shattered over our lives, and we were abandoned by the sun and blown like scattered seed across the Arabian desert, none returned but me, and my Azizya, my precious home, was made to crumble and fall and forever disappear from my life.

And in the words of Jan Wiener, telling of the Nazi invasion of Czechoslovakia, in the book *The Assassination of Heydrich:*

We joined the shocked, silent people in the street. We drifted with them down to Wenceslas Square in the dense, heavy snow. The Square quickly filled with a crowd which stood waiting in silence. Karel Bergmann, Vlasta Chervinka and I stood together, waiting.

When the motorized infantry came, some people thrust their hands into their pockets and only glared, some made threatening gestures with their fists. Many women were crying.

But nobody shouted. Through the steady-falling snowflakes one could hear only the engines. The cold built up inside of us as well as outside as we watched the invaders roll by.

In each of the stories told by my friends, I heard the familiar echo, the thing that held them together. In David Kherdian's words, "The shattered hopes of our orphaned people." The stories themselves, then, were not unique; every family, to some degree, had them. What was unique, I discovered, was the way the storytellers shared them, how they sought to share the spirit of the tale. This was their personal, and communal, triumph: to travel, in storytelling, beyond resignation.

Often, as mythologist and archivist, I have come back to this core truth, the central theme that all is one and one is all. As Larry Littlebird wisely said, we cannot hold on to it all because "it" does not really belong to us. If it belongs to anyone, it is God. And so Larry, through his oral art, chooses to give it back.

From one, truth exfoliates to all. It is our story, then, not yours or his or their story, but all of ours.

Once, a few years ago, I had the chance to share a gathering of Native American oral tales I'd been collecting with a 101-year-old Santo Domingo elder. The old one could not read, so his grandson read my book to him. When he finished reading it aloud, the old man sat in silence for some time. At last he said, "Tell the poet I don't know how he did it, but he hit the true vein. The old ways are still our ways and they will never die." And I thought, when I heard this, Yes, if we—all of us—keep sharing them.

The other day, I heard someone who should have known better say, "Let only those who have lived it tell it." I said to him, "What of those who listen, do they not also experience it, and vicariously live it? Are they not part of the feeling of it?" According to my Navajo friend Ray Brown, when medicine men share a story, an educational process begins that is a circle of sharing between teller and listener. The story is born so that the listener may, at some point, become the teller; and this is how history is written in the human mind, through the power of the whimpering chant.

But Ray also commented, however, that among non-Indians, "there is always a precision to detail, accurateness, and competitiveness," which is why, to a great degree, non-Indians have trouble telling Indian stories. This is not because of ethnic reasons but because of this insistence on detail giving. It is not the detail but the spirit that is worth the detail. In fact, the detail grows out of the spirit, and not the other way around. We need, then, to listen; to begin really to hear what we have only been pretending to hear.

Recently, a Native American friend said, "We are all carriers of water now. Carriers in the desert. We cannot drop even a drop. We must share what we have with everyone. This is the challenge beyond measure." In reaching out through the universality of myth, we should hope to turn hate into love. It is time to stop separating and begin incorporating. Myths and legends, like mountains and rivers, are not things that ought ever to be bought and sold. Nor can they be owned. For as an eighteenth-century elder once said, "The blanket is for all to sit upon." And as another elder said, "If the Great Spirit is always listening, so, my brothers, might we."

Perhaps, in listening, we may, once again, be able to hear. And in having the gift of hearing restored, we may learn to speak what is in each of our hearts. The whimpering chant of human myth brings us together, for we all, regardless of our skin color, have felt shame and sorrow, humility and longing, fear and betrayal. Finally, when we have learned to listen, we may hear that which we say when we say it. And then we will not feel it is necessary to own words, to trap them, to play one against another.

As carriers of water in the desert, we have a great and immeasurable task ahead of us. Let us, each and all, do the carrying well, and not argue about whose hands are on the water jar.

AUTHOR'S NOTE

◆ ◆ ◆

For the last five hundred years, we have called this land America because an Italian explorer who worked for the Spanish Crown made a mistake in geography.

Christopher Columbus, thinking he had come to the East Indies, named the people he saw Indios. One mistake led to another. Columbus's geographical goof awarded the name Indian to a large number of people who already—perhaps for more than ten thousand years—had an abundance of names for themselves. Their names, in their own languages, usually came to be translated into English as The People. Naturally, The Peoples' names are more beautiful in their native tongues, the sounds having a fluency that speaks of the land from which they sprang:

Navajo, Nootka, Oneida, Ojibwa
   Seminole, Seneca
      Shawnee, Shoshone
Hidatsa, Hopi
      Micmac, Miami
Mandan, Kickapoo
Creek, Cayuga
      Umatilla, Paiute
Tuscarora, Wyandot

What a wealth of names The People bequeathed to this nation. And how difficult it is to keep track of them. Consider, for instance, the Chippewa. This name was a corruption of another word, which meant "moccasins with puckered seams." The Chippewa, however, called themselves *Ah-nee-she-nah-be,* or, "first man." In the early 1800s, it was the custom of American settlers to use only the last two syllables of a Native American name. The word *Sioux* was an American corruption of a French corruption of a long Ojibwa name.

And so it went—for centuries.

Perhaps the most regrettable corruption is the name used for this country, America. Originally, this earth, the mother of Native American legend, The People called Turtle Island. And it was thought that the ancient and sacred creature carried the earth upon her back. Turtle was a deity, an ancestor creature, a symbol of long life.

However, Turtle Island was taken from those who named her. And a thing was done that Native Americans have never fully understood: The sacred land was used, sold, bartered, bought and paid for with blood and money. In the end, The People had no part in it, and hardly any place in it. And Mother Earth, Turtle Island, was owned by people who did not seem to know who she was.

The purpose of this book is to take another look at the symbols of the original islanders. How did *they* view the land? They traded names, even sacred ones, so why did they not trade land? Out of Turtle Island came everything necessary, all that was needed for life. *Turtle Island Alphabet* attempts to isolate some of the major recurring themes of native life, and tries to explain their symbolism. Here, then, is an alphabet of terms that dates back ten thousand years. Here are pieces of shell, bits of memory coming from the first days on the Turtle Mother's back, and proceeding into the time of sorrow at the turn of the century, when it seemed that all was lost. Much *was* lost, but the old ways, if they still exist, are present in these symbols, and in the ceremonialism of Native America, which some of us, living and listening, have been fortunate enough to experience—personally, historically, mythically.

ARROW

• • •

During a drought at the Hopi village of Shipaulovi, author Robert Boissiere was asked by his Hopi brother, "Why don't you shoot an arrow straight at the sun? Then we'll have rain."

"I always carried a sixty-pound aluminum steel bow with me," Robert wrote, "to shoot rabbits. Without thinking, I sent an arrow to the sun. No more than three or four minutes elapsed before a cloud darkened over Leslie's field where we were standing; the arrow never came down, but the rain did."

Thus, the arrow can be seen as a symbol for a prayer, the shape of a thought traveling toward a divine destination. So, too, the arrow is tied to the back of the bear in fetishes of the Zuni and other Pueblo people; as if the two, arrow and animal, were in spiritual union, dependent upon one another for life and death.

The arrow is a perfect conception: a thing of beauty, utility, economy, compressed into the most primary shape there is, the straight line. The arrowhead, point of the arrow shaft, is no less lovely in design. Traditionally, it was fashioned of flint, stone, bone, horn, antler, shell, wood, or copper. When the first white Europeans came to the New World, Native Americans began to shape their arrowheads out of iron. The old stone arrowhead, in use for thousands of years, was a greater achievement in terms of craft, however. It also revealed the tribe from which it came: trian-

Arrow-Point Drawings. Mariah Fox. Smithsonian Collection.

Hawk Drawing. Lambert Shaefer.

gular, pointed oval, slender-bladed. Once notched and set into the shaft, the arrowhead was then tied firmly in place with sinew. War arrowheads were loosely attached so the head would remain in the wound; hunting arrowheads were secured so the entire shaft, point included, might later be retrieved.

The arrow, or the shaft, as it is called, was made from reeds, canes, and stems of various kinds of wood. In the Arctic region, owing to the scarcity of material, shafts were made of driftwood. The Plains tribes, and also the Jicarilla Apache, cut shallow grooves lengthwise down the arrow shaft. Referred to as "lightning marks," they were used to keep the arrow's flight true to its mark, to keep the shaft from warping, and to act as a "blood-gutter" once the arrowhead was embedded in its quarry. It was said that an arrow drawn back on the average sixty-pound Native American bow could go through the body of a buffalo.

The arrowhead, as symbol, may be seen on the fetishes of Zuni Pueblo: On the back of the animal fetish, one sees the arrowhead fastened with sinew. The animal ally is joined in spirit with the hunter who seeks its blessing. Thus will the animal come to the hunter swift as a dream, clean as an arrow. The animal, as spirit

Atsina Crazy Dance—The Flight of Arrows. Photograph by Edward S. Curtis. Courtesy Rainbow Man, Santa Fe.

and creature in nature, the arrowhead, and the man are fused into oneness. Here is a ritual in which man and animal participate as equal partners.

A medicine man once compared the "flints of the eagle," its claws, to his own arrow points. The bird of prey, the hunter's heart:

Then the white dream of an arrow
was my own hunger.

Sing thanks for bone, fat, meat
and thong.

Sing praise: my heart, my song.

Through the mystery and passion of the hunt, the Indian put himself on equal footing with his animal brothers. In learning to be one with them, he put himself in their world, which was also his own. The roundness of the bow kept him true to his word as the animals' keeper and friend—but like the bow, he must bend:

From the sun tree he carved an incredible bow that would bend round as the seasons of the sun.
From the moon tree he shaved a flexible arrow that would glow quick as the curve of the moon.

So it was that men, animals, and deities were brought together in the dream of the hunt, the dream of flight, the wisdom of the arrow.

BASKET

◆ ◆ ◆

Years ago, a friend of mine, while climbing a cliff in Arizona, discovered a cave, which, judging by the artifacts around the entrance, had not been entered by a human being for hundreds of years:

Southwest Indian Basket. I.A.I.A. Museum Collection.

Treading darkness
His hand met
The mud-daubed wall
Touched
Palm to palm
The hand made of mud
Left by the cave's
Long gone guardian.
Safe in the hand
Of one whose
Hand was no more,
He heard
The dry bells
Of the rattlesnake
Warning him away.
Backing out of the
Cave, he walked into

The basket of sunlight
Which was
The day he had just
come out of.

When you think of a basket, do you not also think of an offering? The arms that encompass the full basket, the basket of bounty, if you will, are round, as is the basket itself. The beauty of roundness is the earth, and the roundness thereof. In the simplicity of the Native American basket, as a symbol, we do not think of the many styles used by the different tribes (checkerwork, twillwork, wickerwork, wrapped work, twined work); rather, we see the firm work of art, the beauty of round.

That baskets were more than receptacles often escapes the imagination; that basketwork was used for fences, game drives, weirs, houses, shields, clothing, cradles, harvesting, and burial goes beyond the scope we have assigned to the simple basket of our Native American dream world.

In truth, however, the basket may be seen as a weaving, something with warp and weft, something leading all the way to the

Pomo Miniature Baskets. Courtesy W.E. Channing & Co., Santa Fe.

loom. Look at it now—decorated in feather, shell, bead; dyed, plaited, sewed, and embroidered. What a work of art is the basket, and yet the artisan thought not of artistry but of the common balance of utility.

In certain tribal burial rites, the remains of the body (cremated bones, usually) went into or were covered by a basket. In harvest and feast, the basket brought corn and squash, and also served as a cooking implement. Designed with bounty in mind, the open basket is a circle that has neither beginning nor end.

Native American women fashioned baskets of birth, marriage, and death. In the essay "The Basket Maker," first published in 1903, Mary Austin tells of the Paiute woman, Sevayi, who made:

Apache Basket Maker. Photo Number 70/230. Museum of Indian Arts and Culture/Laboratory of Anthropology, Santa Fe.

. . . flaring flat-bottomed bowls, cooking pots really, when cooking was done by dropping hot stones into water-tight food baskets, and for decoration a design in colored bark of the procession of plumed crests of the valley quail. In this pattern she made cooking pots in the golden spring of her wedding year, when the quail went up two and two to their resting places about the foot of Oppapago.

Sevayi made baskets for love and sold them for money, in a generation that preferred iron pots for utility. Every Indian woman is an artist—sees, feels, creates, but does not philosophize about her processes . . . but Sevayi's baskets had a touch beyond cleverness. The weaver and the warp lived next to the earth and were saturated with the same elements. Twice a year, in the time of white butterflies and again when young quail ran neck and neck in the chaparral, Sevayi cut willows for basketry by the creek where it wound toward the river against the sun and sucking winds . . . whenever Sevayi cut willows for baskets was always a golden time, and the soul of the weather went into the wood. If you had ever owned one of Sevayi's golden russet cooking bowls with the pattern of plumed quail, you would understand all this without saying anything.

BEAD

• • •

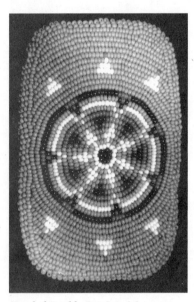

Beaded Buckle. I.A.I.A. Museum Collection.

Native America once produced a wealth, a glorious necklace of beadwork. Today, when it has largely become a salable craft, we may still appreciate the afterglow of its glory. For example, in a single room at Pueblo Bonito, the Hyde Expedition found more than thirty thousand turquoise beads. Before the European-introduced beads of glass and porcelain, Native Americans made beads out of every conceivable thing in the natural world.

There were beads of animal derivation: quill, shell, bone, horn, tooth, claw, tusk. There were vegetal beads of seed, nut, stem, root, plant. Mineral beads of copper, hematite, quartz, serpentine, magnetite, slate, soapstone, and turquoise abounded.

Beauty and money: The Cherokee word for bead and the word for money are the same. The pearl necklace did not come to the Indians from Europe. It was made on Turtle Island. And from the milk tooth of the elk, the canine tooth of the bear, and from birds' beaks and talons came a multitude of lovely beads. What was the purpose of the bead?

Tied into the hair, worn singly on strings, dangling from wrist, waist, and lower limb, the bead made the wearer proud. It celebrated heraldic animals; it told stories and prophesied power; it carried for the wearer an aura of symmetry, suggesting family, tribe, culture. Attractive and precious, sacred and ornamental, the bead was a wealth of things—all of them symbolizing the power of

good health and excellent living. As such, the bead did not represent the material world as much as the nonmaterial one.

The bead, like the basket, is round; and, like the old tribal culture, a single part of many other parts. The string of beads, the blazon of beads told a story in which the single bead was a necessary link to all the others.

One and many: the meaning of the tribe. Together there is strength, unity. The tribal man or woman was as strong as the tribe from which he/she came. And the tribe, naturally, got its strength from the single bead, the pearl, the individual man or woman.

Iroquois Bags. Courtesy W.E. Channing & Co., Santa Fe.

BEAR

◆ ◆ ◆

Zuni Bear Fetish. Sue Kehe.
Courtesy Sunstone Press.

The bear is one of the most potent Native American symbols. But it should be noted, as I once wrote in the book *Meditations with Animals,* that "Bears have both good and bad power. A spirit unruly and wild, human and divine." Navajo legends are replete with bear stories that reflect the duality of bear power. Characteristically, the bear "must be brought to earth in spirit, tamed . . . ." Otherwise, he/she may represent "that side of us which is inclined to do harm." In some Native American bear rituals, the animal's dual nature becomes the power that heals:

Sitting on the Blue-Eyed Bear

Inside the hogan
colored earths make bear tracks
leading in,
bear tracks and sunlight—
sun dogs
at the four quarters.
Bear is soaked in sunlight
in the center.
Twigs at the entrance of Bear's den
are trees.

The sick person has a vision of Bear
when he sits upon painted sand.
Then Bear-man
rushes into the hogan, snarling and growling.
All the sitting people join in—
this is the moment
when the women faint.

The preceding poem comes from the Navajo Mountain Top
Way, which, translated directly, means "a chant toward a place
within the mountains." The Bear People, once banished to live in
isolation at Black Mountain, are the main force behind the
Mountain Top Way. In the old healing chants of this Way, Bear-
man and Snake-man were appointed guardians of Sun's House.
Changing Woman (Earth Mother deity of the Navajo) had given
Bear as a gift to The People, but he and Snake-man showed an
inclination to align themselves with "the dark side" and were, in
the end, banished. One of Bear's illnesses, passed on to The People
as a result of his commingling with them, is coughing (bears
always cough or woof when you come upon them in the forest).

The poem also mentions the shock rite, wherein Bear-man
enters the hogan and the women faint. Another adverse aspect of
Bear, in Navajo religion, is that in their ancient past, a primary sister turned into a Bear Person who seduced her brothers with
magic and subsequently killed them. The purpose of the shock rite
is to induce and correct the symptoms brought on by all of Bear's
malign influences. Supernatural beings, such as Bear and Snake, if
contemplated—by their very nature, which is powerful—can
cause sickness. In this particular rite, the illness is suddenly and
dramatically drawn out of the patient.

The purpose of the Mountain Top Way is to remove the ill
effects caused by the Bear People. The Way cures disease and
invokes unseen power on behalf of The People, for bringing rain
and nurturing healthy crops. By sitting on the sand painting

Look at the Butterfly. Beatian Yazz.
Courtesy Sunstone Press.

described in the poem, the patient draws forth strength, and is thus healed. The Mountain Top Way can be done only in winter when Thunder is still and Rattlesnake is hibernating. To perform the ritual at any other time could bring death from lightning or snakebite. (The relationship between the two latter deities—one an agent of earth power, the other its reflection in the sky—is discussed in greater detail in the story "Zigzag" on page 196.)

BLANKET

◆ ◆ ◆

One of the standard icons of western Americana is the portrait of the Noble Red man with the blanket thrown over one shoulder. During the nineteenth century, this image was so common that Indians who refused to accept "modern dress" were known as Blanket Indians. Before the blanket, as we know it today, Indians wore robes made from the whole hide of an animal—or many hides sewn together. Woven robes were used by Indians long before the advent of the loom. Made from feathers, hair, fur, down, bark, and cotton, these items were used ceremonially, as well as for bed coverings, wall hangings, doors, awnings, and sunshades.

With the appearance of commercial woolen blankets, and as fur became scarce in the American West, Indians took pleasure in manufactured blankets. During the nineteenth century, delegations of tribal people went to Washington, D. C., wearing the standard Native American uniform, the blanket.

In the Southwest, the coming of the Spaniards brought wide-spread blanket making. First the Pueblo, then the Navajo got sheep and looms from the Spanish. The Navajo sheared their own sheep, washed the wool, colored it with native dyes, and spun it on spindles. The coarse and uneven yarn was then set up in a loom. Among the Pueblo, the men did the weaving. The Navajo reversed the process, and, in time, created some of the finest blankets ever woven.

Navajo Rug. I.A.I.A. Museum Collection.

Among the Hopi, a white cotton wedding blanket is woven by the groom for his bride. At death, this blanket is wrapped about her body in preparation for last rites. In traditional Navajo blankets that show images from sacred sand paintings, there is always a space woven into the blanket wherein the visiting *yei*, the holy people, the subjects of the blanket and its central imagery, may "escape back to their world." Thus, they are there on the blanket, but they can leave at will. The blanket's conception is, therefore, "real" rather than imagined.

Growing up in a house full of Navajo blankets, some of them quite rare, I was glad that my mother believed they were meant to be used, not stored away or hung on the wall for decoration. The most valuable Navajo weaving our family had was a "crystal blanket." Because it was too heavy and coarse for bedding, too beautiful to put on the floor, my mother used it as a kind of traveling blanket. It went with us, moving from place to place, often on camping trips, but usually it was an "art blanket." This meant my mother, who was an artist, liked to use it to sit on when she was doing an oil painting outdoors.

The blanket, which my mother gave to my wife for a wedding present, is still somehow sweet-scented with the old Navajo richness of unrefined wool. There is a desert smell about it, something of the weaver and the distant past—a place of beginnings, no longer there. Of course, it always reminds me of childhood. I think of mornings when, seated on the blanket's golden-headed crows, I watched my brother carve coral snakes out of wood and paint them red and yellow. Remembering that, I can hear the rhyme he used to recite.

It told of the design on a coral snake's back: Red and yellow will kill a fellow. And the other pattern that belonged to the harmless king snake: Red and black is okay for Jack. On the safe margin of that mystic blanket, I learned to say the rhyme of life and death— sitting on the crystal crows of harmony in a gold Navajo dawn.

Above: Navajo Rug. Courtesy W.E. Channing & Co., Santa Fe.

Opposite: Santa Clara Pueblo Girl. Photograph by Joe Hedrick.

BUFFALO

◆ ◆ ◆

Strike our land with your great curved horns
In anger, toss the turf in the air.
Now strike our land
With your great curved horns.
We will hear the song
And our hearts will be strong . . .
      —traditional song of the Chippewa

My mother used to tell of the one-horse sleigh her father had
when she was a girl. The family would ride in the sleigh, buried
deep under a buffalo robe, bells ringing as the runners of the
sleigh hissed upon the crisp new-fallen snow. The buffalo robe,
mantle of the Plains Indians, was the ubiquitous winter blanket of
the West. My mother used to say there was nothing warmer, nothing more comforting against the cold. She said it was as if the great
buffalo were still alive, sharing its great, ungainly body heat.

To the American Indian, the buffalo was an elder, a teacher. It
taught all manner of men, but its innermost secrets were revealed
only to medicine men. To them, it explained where to find medicinal plants. From the animal's habits and movements came the
shapes and names of the Plains Indians' months. The buffalo,
horned and shag-headed, was symbol of the leader, image of long
life, abundance, and power. Ceremonies of the Plains tribes were
held in the buffalo's honor and myths were made of its history on
earth.

Arikara Medicine Ceremony—The Buffalo. Photograph by Edward S. Curtis. Courtesy Rainbow Man, Santa Fe.

In the last quarter of the nineteenth century, the deathblow of the great herds—brought on by white westward expansion—heralded the extinction of the tribes themselves. Their dependence upon the buffalo for physical and spiritual blessing gave them reason to live. Without the buffalo, the months were meaningless, the days were without design.

In the poem "Buffalo Dance at Cochiti," poet-anthropologist Phillips Kloss speaks of the perfection he witnessed on a "clear warm Christmas morning" many New Mexico years ago.

Buffalo Dance at Cochiti

It was the young Buffalo Mother who focalized and inspired it,
    exquisite grace in every movement of her lithe slender
    body, carved consecration on her beautiful Indian face.

The rhythm of her footsteps seemed a separate song over the
    drum-beat, sometimes one foot suspended gliding back

and forth, the other pulsing up and down, alternating, a
   most subtle syncopation,

A superb arm gesture, right hand upraised majestic, swooping
   down like a rush of rain, pulling up like growing corn,
   symbol of fertility.

She drew the dance pattern around her like the design of an old
   Cochiti waterjar, the two buffalo-headed male dancers
   diagonalled away from her, circled back, the little antelope
   dancers with stiff stick forelegs aligned horned-headed
   toward her.

She drew the landscape around her, the river valley, the cliffcave
   canyons, tent rocks, pines, junipers, manzanita, dahlia,
   ephedra,
Forgotten meanings reanimated in the dance, hovering over it
   almost tangible.

That the whites played sport with the great herds, shooting
them for tongue, filet, and hide, was worse than tragedy. Beyond
this, it speaks of genocide, because the U.S. government knew that
by silencing the herds, the Indians would soon follow. It is all a
strange, blurred, and painful tale, often told, frequently misunderstood. There was room for everybody, some of the elders said.
There was not room, however, for people who pushed other people out. So there was war, and there were broken vows. The buf-
faloes and the Indians faded upon the plain and the white man put
up fences for cattle. This, according to Oren Lyons, faithkeeper of
the Onandaga, brought the whole thing down: the true death of
the Indian nations.
   The present species of buffalo, *Bison americanus,* once ranged
freely between the Rocky and the Allegheny mountains. In 1530,
when the first explorer made mention of seeing a buffalo, the

herds ranged across most of North America. In fact, they roamed as far north as British Columbia and as far south as Louisiana. The tribes—and they were numerous—that lived within the buffalo's range were dependent upon it for food, clothing, shelter, and religion.

Early accounts of Native American buffalo hunts related different styles of hunting, including driving the herd to a designated area by lighting fire to the prairie, and driving them into pens, off cliffs, and into rivers. Tribal buffalo hunts were ceremonial and often included the entire tribe. In such a circumstance, the penalty for hunting the buffalo singly was death.

Buffalo hunts usually occurred in June, July, and August, when the buffalo were fat, their fur was thin, and their flesh was excellent for eating. In winter, when the hunting parties were small, the pelts were used for bedding, tepee covers, and moccasins. Early winter and autumn were the best times to get a buffalo robe, for the fur was richest then. In addition to the meat and hide, the Indians used other parts of the buffalo. The tallow was kept in skin bags, as was the marrow. The sinew was kept for bowstrings, rope, and thread. The horns were made into spoons and drinking vessels. The droppings were used for fuel. Nothing was wasted.

Some writers have speculated that the Plains tribes loved the buffalo to such a degree that when it was decimated by the onrush of white hunters, they believed something much worse would come. This was not death, for they had always lived with that. It was rather a kind of living death.

The penned livestock that replaced the great herds, the horizon line of telegraph wires, and steaming trains were less fearful to the Indian than the rumor that something worse was on its way.

And what has happened? What has changed?

Nothing really. The rape of Mother Earth continues along on its unchecked course. Devastators more dreadful than the grinning, stalking buffalo hunters have come and gone, and have been replaced by newer and more phantasmagorical levelers of the

Red Buffalo. Acrylic. Kate Krasin. Courtesy Sunstone Press.

landscape. The evil that the Indians felt was coming has not yet come. Patience, it will arrive soon. We await the hour of Armageddon, that "rough beast" of W. B. Yeats's fearful poem, "The Second Coming."

So it is not what comes but what *is* coming that makes for troubled sleep. The white man, ever moving forward, never looking back, is now the inheritor of his progress: an illness that kills. The Pueblo poet Harold Littlebird, speaking as universal conscience, says in his own way that we—whoever, whatever we are—cannot turn away from ourselves, our true nature.

Hands That Kiss the Earth

Hands that kiss the Earth,
  that know the rain,
Hands that held the clouds,
  that smelled the sun,
    Hands of your breath,
    that sang your song
folded over my eyes
  and landed on my heart.
You soared like the eagle
  and slept in me
with your full awareness
  of my being and your
  full awareness of you.
  I am the deer you hunt.
I am the rain you chase. I am You.

CAMP

◆ ◆ ◆

Home, for the first European settlers in America, was a kind of camp. Then, as time went on, camp turned into cabin. And cabin became the village, which, in less than one hundred years, mushroomed into the busy city that Carl Sandburg once sang about. "City of the big shoulders," he called it, pointing out in the poem "Chicago" that, under the glare of the streetlight, the prostitute waited for the farmboy, fresh in from the country.

City of workers and dreams, and flying machines.

City of smoked glass and sleeked steel.

City of babies and burdens, and broken dreams.

So it was not so long before the rhapsody of camp and cabin came back into the American imagination, as it will every century or so, reclaiming the soil, the so-called heartland of the good life. And with nostalgia running in their veins, Americans will again look back with longing to the mountains and rivers, prairies and valleys that they gave up and left behind in their search for a brighter future. So the cycle goes, growing and dreaming and leaving and dreaming, and eventually, but usually too late, returning.

But what of the natives of Turtle Island? Did they return, in dream, to the lost land of their birth?

Did they cry out after what was lost? Or did they shrink in sorrow, and try to forget?

We sometimes think of them—after the reservations were in

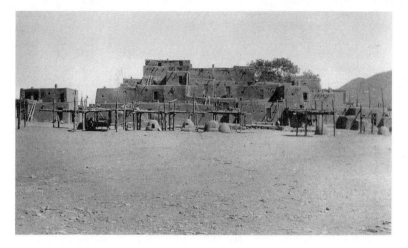

Taos Pueblo. Courtesy Roy Wright.

place—as mute sufferers. The scars too deep, the suffering too great to bear witness in words to what had truly happened, what was truly lost. There was no room here for nostalgia; leave that to the people who had lost nothing—who could always go back, if they chose to.

But yes, the Indian people sang of the things they had once done, the beauty betrayed, and it is still some of the best poetry ever to appear. One thinks of Black Elk on his mountain, the tears streaming down his face, his vision broken, the good, red road of peace destroyed:

> I did not know then how much was ended. When I look back now from this high hill of my old age, I can still see the butchered women and children lying heaped and scattered all along the crooked gulch as plain as when I saw them with eyes still young.

Or, as Sitting Bull said at the very end:

> A warrior I have been
> Now
> It is all over

A hard time
I have.

And the song of the Ghost Dance, the religion which was to
have danced back the buffalo and given the Indian his rightful
place under the sun:

My children, I, when at first I liked the whites
My children, I, when at first I liked the whites
I gave them fruits
I gave them fruits.

Father have pity on me
Father have pity on me
I am crying for thirst
I am crying for thirst
All is gone—I have nothing to eat.

The song of the open land, the return to camp and cabin, tepee
and tent comes back every fifty years or so for all of those among
us who can feel the old ways in the blood. In America, we have
had a number of these Mother Earth revivals, not the least of
which is the one going on right now—not to celebrate—but to
save her. In the sixties, thirty years ago, a less frenetic program of
earth saving was taking place: the romance to return to a tribal
community.

But around the turn of the century, the first of these revivals of
the good, remembered years was happening. Writers and artists
such as Ernest Thompson Seton, Dan C. Beard, Frederic
Remington, Charley Russell, and American Indian spokespeople
such as George Bird Grinnell, Black Elk, and others were telling us
that it was already getting late, the time had come to save what was
being swept away.

In the 1930s, yet another paean to native tradition and to

Mother Earth was seen in both the literary and visual arts. During this era and for the next twenty years, some of the best Native American poetry, prose, and music was recorded and published. And ethnographic writers and artists, Elsie Clews Parsons and Gene Kloss, to name just two, saved, in word and art, the old ways that were being forgotten on the reservation.

In the 1960s, as previously mentioned, the American youth movement began the revival that is continuing today. For the first time in more than one hundred years, Native American authors took up the pen and stood before the podium to make the other half, the missing half, of the story known. Vine Deloria, Jr., N. Scott Momaday, James Welch, Leslie Marmon Silko, and many others began to tell the story again, but from a new yet ancient and immemorial perspective.

This is how it is, they said, this is how it has come to be what it is, based upon what it once was. The old earth, the people on it; those who love it, those who try to destroy it.

The old, the oldest story.

Now, in the 1990s, the questions come without end. As we near the cycle of five hundred years since Columbus blundered into historical tragedy, many people want to know what happened, how did the land get ruined so fast, what did this nation do to hasten the destruction. Who owned the land in the first place? Did each tribe lay claim to a certain territorial part of it? And did they really think they "owned" the land? How did they look at Turtle Island? Was it theirs, by birthright? Did they believe that it belonged to the deities who permitted them to hunt and plant and walk upon it? These are the old unresolved questions of ownership.

In a sense (innocence), the Turtle Islanders borrowed the land; they claimed title to its use by taking up a part of it. Each tribe used a certain locality as its preferred habitat. The gatherers of acorns, seeds, and roots made their mark on the places that suited them best, and they camped around them for a season before moving on to another place. The catchers of salmon or other fish knew where their quarry lived and they camped around the streams, rivers, and brooks and made their seasonal homes there. The hunters of game made makeshift shelters or lived in portable dwellings for the part of the year that called them to the places of the hunt. And thus the people lived, part of each year, where the living was best for them. Their homes were brush shelters, mat houses, bark lodges, and skin tents.

Rush-mat houses, woven by women, were rolled into a bundle for easy moving. When they got to their camping place, they made an oblong frame of tied-together saplings, and this was their temporary home. The Plains people who lived in skin tents, known generally as tepees, cut and trimmed ten to twenty lodge poles for each one. The tanning, cutting, fitting, and sewing of the tepee, generally made of buffalo skin, was the work of the women. The poles and skins were dragged from place to place, first by dogs, travois-style, and later by horses.

The details of tepee camp were controlled by the women, except in the case of war parties, where the men did the organization and work. Tepees were usually set up in a circle, the closest of kin being the closest neighbor. If danger from enemies was expected, horses and all valuable possessions were kept within the space enclosed by the tepees. Sometimes the camp was in concentric circles, each circle representing a political group. The Dakota called themselves "Seven Council Fires." They camped in two groups: one composed of four concentric circles and one of three concentric circles. The Omaha camped in a circle and each of the ten clans had its special place. The tribal circle of tepee life was a living picture of the way the tribe functioned, how it worked as a whole. Order from within and protection from without is still the basic premise of tent camping today. The tenets of the Boy Scouts were gratefully borrowed by Ernest Thompson Seton from various Indian tribes with whom he was acquainted. His own experiences with tent living, camping, woodcraft, and sign language sprang from encounters

Lone Tree Lodge—Ticarilla.
Photograph by Edward S. Curtis.
Courtesy Rainbow Man, Santa Fe.

with Native Americans at the turn of the century.

And so the story ends: the borrowers, the Indians, were borrowed from by the white man and not paid back. The grievous loan is still outstanding.

White America, however, cannot return what it took because what is gone is not returnable—it is gone forever. Nor can the culture at large ever atone, or even attempt to atone, for what was done a century ago. As Black Elk put it: ". . . the nation's hoop is broken and scattered. There is no center any longer, and the sacred tree is dead."

We must, if we are to continue to live, treasure what we have, not pine uselessly for what we have lost. We cannot go back. We must go on, resourcefully. As one Native American said recently, "We are all carriers of water, now. Carriers in the desert. We cannot drop even a drop. We must share what we have with everyone. This is the challenge beyond measure."

CORN

◆ ◆ ◆

He saw again the bodies bent in the sun,
The dark skin and water-black hair.
He heard again the rising song of the earth
The People singing alongside the ears
Of corn, the men and women and children
Coming out of the earth like the corn,
The song of the corn.
—*From a conversation with* JAY DE GROAT

It was called maize, from the Arawak Indian word *marise*. It sprang, so it is thought today, from native grasses of southern Mexico and Guatemala. Linguistic evidence points to the fact that maize came to Turtle Island from the tribes of Mexico and from the Carib of the West Indies. The ease with which maize could be cultivated made it very accessible to tribes all over North America. In 1586, a visitor to Virginia saw that the Indians put four grains in a hill "with care that they not touch one another." In 1687, another observer saw that more than a million bushels of Iroquois corn were destroyed by a military maneuver: It took the army seven days to cut up the corn of only four Indian villages.

From what later came to be known as Indian corn, there were derived the following foods: ash cake, hoecake, succotash, and hominy. The concept of the southern corncrib was originally borrowed from the southern Indians.

In the Hopi Butterfly Dance, the voices sing:

We are young
　The corn is green
We chase the yellow sun
We play with golden
　　　Butterfly girls.

Southwest Symbol. I.A.I.A.
Museum Collection.

Throughout the Southwest, the tribes revere the single stalk of female blessing. There is the Santo Domingo Corn Dance, wherein the entire tribe dances in the golden sun for the greatness of the harvest, the goodness of the corn. In the sand paintings of the Navajo, the corn people and The People themselves are indistinguishable: Human figures and cornstalks are interchangeable forms of life. They stand erect, in twos and fours, the men with round heads, the females with square.

Jay de Groat expresses this well in the poem "His Children":

His Children

my father blessed it "with beauty before me"
　as he sowed the seeds
　　yellow corn my sister
　　white corn　my brother
　in mother earth's womb

my father sheltered and prayed "with beauty under me"
　as he witnessed the growth
　　each uniquely its own
　　as leaves moved leisurely
　with mother earth's breath

my father perceived promise "with beauty around me"
　as he touched the ripener
　　uncomparable beauty

and intricate
  by mother earth's workmanship

my father was blissful "with beauty behind me"
  as he harvested the crop
    yellow corn
    white corn
  from mother earth's bosom

my father is content "with beauty it is done"
  as he acknowledges
    individual beauty that came
    through him but not from him
  his children

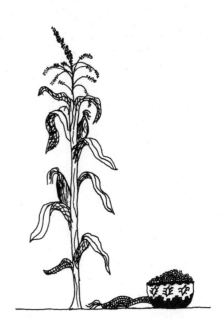

It is corn pollen and cornmeal that is given in blessing and in ceremony to protect, to understand, and to ask forgiveness. Corn, the everlasting mother. From the jungles of Mexico to the heights of Hopi, it is corn, the guardian. As Frank Waters writes in *Masked Gods: Navajo and Pueblo Ceremonialism:*

Thus, as in Taos, the perfect ears of corn, those without blemish, and with the tips ending in four kernels, are saved for kiva ceremonials and are called Corn Mothers. With fire, feathers and water, corn takes its place in the kiva as one of the major symbols of the four worlds, often synonymous with the earth itself.

CRADLE

◆ ◆ ◆

It is said that the first American lullabies came from cradlesongs sung by American Indian mothers to their young ones. The following lullaby comes from the Cheyenne:

> Little good baby,
>   hey-ye
> Sleepy little baby.
>   A-ha, hm.

In the country of cold and the country of warm, and all points in between, Native Americans made cradles for their infants. These functioned as both carrier and carriage and were made of bark, skin, and woven wood. Skin cradles made from buffalo hide with the fur side facing in were used by the Plains tribes. Bark cradles, used in the interior of Alaska, were constructed of a single piece of birch or other bark bent into the form of a trough, with a hood adorned with quillwork. The bed was soft fur and the cradle was carried on the mother's back by means of a forehead band.

Plains Indians also made lattice cradles. These were made of dressed skins lashed to a lattice of flat sticks. The infant, wrapped in furs, was entirely encased. Over the face of the cradle was bent a flat bow, hung with pendants and amulets, and covered with a

In the Cradle-Basket. Photograph by Edward S. Curtis. Courtesy Rainbow Man, Santa Fe.

hood. The frame was carried on the mother's back or swung from the pommel of a saddle.

Pawnee cradle boards came from the "heart" of trees specially selected for this purpose. The thought behind this was that the tree's heart and the child's were inextricably bound. The head of the cradle was designed to follow the grain of the wood; the spotted bobcat or lynx skin that served as cover symbolized the stars, while the cradle's bow represented the sky, and the crooked furrow carved in it was the lightning.

Comanche Mothers. Photograph by Edward S. Curtis. Courtesy Rainbow Man, Santa Fe.

Hammock cradles were often made of woven wood and they were designed to be hung at the ends. This was a true "sleeping cradle," or rather, a "carrying cradle."

Among Pueblo people, the cradle was a sacred object. Handed down from one generation to the next, the number of children that slept in it were notched on the frame. To sell such a valuable and spiritual object would cause the death of the child who was using it. However, if the infant died of natural causes during the time the cradle was being used, it was then broken up, burned, placed on the grave, or disposed of in some other way.

The Kwakiutl cradle was hung from a cross beam in a corner of the house. A cord, attached to the cradle, was gently pulled to and fro by the mother as she sang her child a lullaby.

Adults, too, had a kind of cradle and cradlesong to go with it. The Cheyenne, for instance, made swings of buffalo-hide strips, which they hung from the boughs of trees. Men, women, and children would ride the swing as members of the tribe sang them a traditional swinging song that beckoned the wood rats to draw near. (Wood rats, or "timbermen," as they were called, were good to eat but hard to catch. The people sang to them to come while the swings moved to and fro.)

The Pawnee legend of the Morning Star tells of the cradle board hanging upon posts in the lodge of the heavens. Thus the child of the Pawnee carries the Morning Star on its cradle board and lives under the protection of this star.

Rock-a-bye baby
On the tree top
When the wind blows
The cradle will rock
When the bough breaks
The cradle will fall
And down will come baby,
Cradle and all

Joseph Bruchac, the Abenaki storyteller, once told me that this most famous American lullaby was "borrowed" by a Puritan from one of the Algonquin-speaking nations of New England. The beauty, simplicity, and, perhaps, irony are serenely Native American, as is the cradle hung upon a star at the stairway of the wind. May the song and the cradle be returned to its rightful owner.

DANCE

◆ ◆ ◆

Sia (Zia) War Dancer. Photograph by Edward S. Curtis. Courtesy Rainbow Man, Santa Fe.

The oldest dance on earth
Begins and ends
With the heart.
No saying can enter
The sun wind, the hawk look
The coyote foot,
The ancestor heart
Forever beating back.

We run on the coiled clay shards
Of those who were once
Formed by sun, cloud, sand—
Who came out of the earth.

We run on the shapely bones
Of those who were once
Like us, the runners,
With feet of dust.

The oldest dance on earth is the dance of the hunter, chanter, singer, and lover. And it is the dance of the dancer: the expression of universal exuberance, love of life. The Native American dance, then, can be seen as a prayer expressing the relationship between the nonphysical and the physical world. The mystic meaning of the dancer, runner, lover, hunter is the same. Interestingly, the Natchez Indians used the same love charm to call a deer to the bow and a woman to the bed.

Just as "the word was God," so, too, the dance was, and is, the setting of that word into physical motion. Thus, dance is inseparable from song, chant, prayer. The dancing heart of the hunter reaches out to the hunted, and they are one. The tribal dance is, therefore, an expression of union with the deities.

Native American dances and the customs contained within them are too complicated to pare down and discuss in a few short paragraphs. There are the dances of clans, societies, as well as tribes. There are the dances of one sex and not the other, and the dances of both sexes. There are social dances, erotic dances, comic, mimic, and patriotic dances. There are the dances of offering, mourning, and ancient memory.

The Seneca had, for instance, thirty-two leading dances, of which six might be called "costume dances," fourteen were for men and women together, eleven were for men only, and seven were for women only. Three of the costume dances were exclusively for men, while three were reserved for both sexes.

Generally speaking, dance postures of Native Americans may be divided into male and female categories. Traditionally, the woman's role is earthly, passive, and slower in movement than the man's. Dancing women often resemble a wind-rocked stalk of corn. In fact, among the Onondaga, Cayuga, and other Iroquois tribes, one of the names for woman was *wathonwisas,* which means "she sways or rocks."

The man's role is freer, less earthbound, perhaps more imitative of animal and other deities. As the woman is the earth, the man is the sky, and therefore the dance steps of each take power from their respective sources of energy.

Native American dances often circulate, so to speak, around the sun. Thus they are sunwise, earth-round, seasonal expressions of

Pueblo Dancer. Waldo Mootzka (Hopi artist). Courtesy W.E. Channing & Co., Santa Fe.

Apache Crown Dancers. Photo Number 70/198. Museum of Indian Arts and Culture/Laboratory of Anthropology, Santa Fe.

devotion. Among the Muskogean tribes, the dance circles move in opposite directions: the men with the course of the sun, the women contrary to it. Natchez dancers moved thus: women turning from left to right, men turning from right to left. The dance movement from right to left was designed so that the male dancer did not turn his back to the sun.

Not long ago, my friend Sol Hill came back from Zuni pueblo, where the Shalako dances were again opened to the public. Peering in the windows of adobe houses, he witnessed the tall, masked dancers, kachinas, with their medieval birds' beaks, clapping—*pom, pom, pom*—to the metronomic heartbeat of the drum. As he watched in the December night frost, he said that his heart was taught the monosyllabic beat of the desert drum. Magically, he was not cold anymore. One with the drum, his breath making feather puffs before his eyes, he watched the dance of the Shalako, and listened to the boom of the bird-foot drum. He was outside the wall, a stranger. And at the same time, he found himself inside the warm fire-lit family room where the gawky and odd seven-foot bird, headdress of buffalo wool and eagle feather, danced its dance, godlike re-creation of the meeting of sky and earth.

DOLL

◆ ◆ ◆

In Santa Fe, New Mexico, where tourists come from all over the world to buy Native American art and artifacts as well as crafts, cottonwood kachina dolls carved by Pueblo and Navajo artisans are collectible art forms. The average tourist buys them without knowledge of what they are, what they represent; few know what the word *kachina* really means. In Hopi, *kachi* means life or spirit and *Na* means Father. *Kachi-na,* therefore, is not a doll, as Americans understand the meaning of that word. Rather, it is an embodiment of the spirit of love, power, and wisdom emanating from the actual deity, the kachina: Life-Father, Spirit-Father, Father-Spirit. As a Hopi potter once said, "We potters are respectful of our clay, for some of it may contain the dust of our ancestors."

Native American "dolls" are of two types: ceremonial objects and children's toys, which, nonetheless, may also be ceremonial or instructional in nature. For instance, kachina dolls, as such, were designed for the edification of children, not merely as objects of play. As one writer put it, Hopi kachina dolls are the impersonation of ancestral "breath bodies."

The dolls, the writer went on to say, were not worshiped. They were made by kiva priests during the great spring ceremonies and given to little girls on the morning of the last day of the festival by men in kachina costume, who were themselves physical imperson-

Hopi White Buffalo Kachina.
I.A.I.A. Museum Collection.

ations of the kachina spirit. In this manner, the young people of the tribe became familiar with its deities, customs, dances, and ceremonials.

Eskimo dolls of the dead were used in a festival of homage in which the dolls were placed before the feast. As the life spirits of the dead, these dolls commemorated the ancestors' time on earth. Iroquois dolls of dough were ceremonial, while those that were made by and for children to play with were constructed of corn-cob and rag.

A child playing sees us coming, cries.
Moccasined mother chases after her,
Turquoise squash blossom
   banging at her breast.

The child is swooped up.
Eyes of unseen things sparkle back
From sky-roof antlers:
The child's cornhusk doll, eyeless
   grinning in the dust.

Opposite: Hopi Kachinas (carved from cottonwood). Courtesy W.E. Channing & Co., Santa Fe.

Above: Hopi Kachina Doll in Deer Dance Stance. I.A.I.A. Museum Collection.

EAGLE

◆ ◆ ◆

Once, at dusk, along the western edge of the Rio Grande Gorge, I caught two eagles doing a kind of mating dance in midair. First, they were two birds on the wing, then they merged into one. As one tilted up in the downdraft of the canyon, the other went down. Soon I was lost in their flight across the empty air, and they had become not birds of prey but the deep canyon itself; their wings, now walls, roughed and rocked, closed in until I was safe in their dream, close in canyon quiet:

> His right wing o p e n e d
>   to the West
>
> Feathers pointed North
>
> Wind from the East
>   over the dunes
>   from the steadfast mountains
>   making his feathers
>   wrap around his sandy face
>   like human hair
>   over a goddess's cheek

The deep Blue of evening
Captured in the sheen of feathers made
This Turquoise wing cradle
  his white head
    and
  yellow beak
  as he spoke

    —Loren Straight Eagle Plume

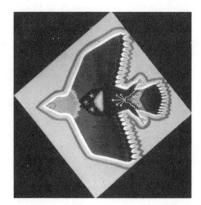

I.A.I.A. Museum Collection.

Of all birds that figure in Native American mythology, the most seminal is the eagle. The solitary mystery and power of this bird, as perceived by the Indian, was immediately grasped by the emerging nation of the United States, and used for its emblem.

The bird, as symbol and sacrificial/ceremonial presence, has always belonged, and rightfully so, to the American Indian, however. It is ironic that today the bald eagle is an endangered species—made so not by the Indian but by white American hunters. Yet, as ever, the Indian must suffer, dyeing goose feathers to look like eagle plumes for sacred ceremonies, because the America that killed off the eagle now desperately wants it back.

Naturally, like the buffalo, the eagle was used by the Indian for a myriad of things. The wing bones were made into whistles, carried by warriors, used in ceremonies. Medicine men also used eagle-bone "sucking tubes" to draw out illness or disease. The talons were used for amulets, fetishes, and necklaces. The capture of eagles for feathers, feet, and claws was a rite of passage for many young men. Here, for example, is a "winter count," a way of marking time for certain Plains tribes; this winter count is rendered into words from a pictograph on a buffalo hide:

Man who digs hole and covers himself
reaches out when eagle falls

Eagle Dance—San Ildefonso.
Photograph by Edward S. Curtis.
Courtesy Rainbow Man, Santa Fe.

and takes eagle by feet—
this man is an eagle,
now joined are head and claw!

Robert Boissiere writes of Kwahu, the ceremonial eagle, pinioned to a log on the roof of his Hopi brother's mesatop house at Shipaulovi:

Each clan member at Hopi had the right to catch a young eagle in the spring in the cliffs surrounding the mesas, sometimes forty or fifty miles away. Each Hopi clan had ancestral eagle nests reserved for the members of a particular clan. Because of the sacredness of the magnificent bird, it would bless a household by its very presence, becoming, in actuality, a member of the family. . . .

Boissiere goes on to explain that after a specific measure of time, the eagle is sacrificed "after being blessed and loaded with messages to take to the spirit world." And so, he says, "it remains with its Hopi brothers forever."

It was once spoken among the Plains Indians that the price of twelve feathers—white plume, black tip—from the war eagle (the golden eagle) was worth the price of a horse. Eagle feathers among the different tribes represented certain kinds of status. It was the custom of the Pillager Chippewa to permit a warrior who scalped an enemy to wear two eagle feathers. The act of capturing a wounded prisoner on the battlefield earned the distinction of five feathers. Fans made of the primary feathers of the eagle were—and are still—used for ceremonial purposes. As ornaments on buckskin shirts worn by men, the eagle feather was worn by various tribes. In addition, it was depicted, as symbol, on shields, pottery, beadwork, quillwork, and cloth. The emblem eagle is also seen on totem poles, houses, and grave posts of North Pacific tribes. The Tlingit sprinkled eagle down on hair, masks, and dance costumes. Pueblo Indians of the Southwest wear headdresses with the same ceremonial sprinkling, which Frank Waters comments on in *Masked Gods: Navajo and Pueblo Ceremonialism,* stating that these bits of fluff may also represent the coming of snow, a blessing for crops in spring.

Near the Hopi villages, there are shrines in which carved wooden replicas of eagle eggs are placed during the winter solstice as a prayer for the fecundity of eagles. Among the Zuni, plucked feathers have a value different from eagle feathers that fall naturally from the bird.

In many tribes, there are myths relating to the eagle god, eagle beings, thunderbirds. A Navajo ceremonial speaks of the first eagle slain by Elder Brother, one of the tribe's primary deities. After killing the mother and father eagle, he adopts the nestlings for the tribe, for The People:

From this day forward you will not think
as your father thought . . . or your mother.
You nestlings belong to The People now.
They will wear your claws
 dance with your feathers
   see with your eyes.
      You belong to The People.

FEATHER

♦ ♦ ♦

For decorations of war, worship, and as an expression of flight, the feather is the universal Native American symbol. In Arctic regions, the Indian sought water birds. On the North Pacific coast, they captured or killed ravens and flickers. In California, the tribes hunted woodpeckers, meadowlarks, crested quail, mallard ducks, blue jays, blackbirds, and orioles. Around the southwestern pueblos, hunters went after eagles, hawks, turkeys, and parrots. Using the feathers and skins and even bodies of birds, the tribes made clothes, masks, hats, blankets, and robes.

Parkas in the Arctic were made of water-bird skins sewn together, the feathers acting as insulation and waterproofing. Tribes to the south used the skins of young waterfowl, while still downy, and sewed them into robes. Eastern tribes cut bird skins into strips and wove them into blankets in the same way that western tribes used rabbit skins.

Captain John Smith and other early European settlers observed that the Indians of the East fashioned turkey robes: feathers tied in knots to form a network out of which beautiful patterned cloaks were wrought.

Fans and other accessories of dress were made of wings or feathers by the Iroquois. The western Eskimo sewed little sprays of down into the seams of garments. California tribes decorated their basketry with feathers; quills of small birds were incorporated into

Plains Pipe. Billy Joe Jackson, Sioux. I.A.I.A. Museum Collection.

Serpent. Alexander Garcia, San Juan Pueblo. I.A.I.A. Museum Collection.

basketry in much the same way as porcupine quills. Of course, one of the most common uses of the feather was in arrow making. For giving directness in flight, arrow feathers were split so that halves could be glued to the shaft of the arrow in twos and threes.

An unusual use of bird scalps was practiced by certain California tribes, who used them as money, being both a standard of value and a medium of exchange.

The down feathers of birds have a special value to Native Americans. Light and airy, fluffy and snowy, these feathers can be seen as a bridge between the spirit world and Mother Earth, or simply as messenger and prayer feathers. *Pahos,* as they are called among the Hopi, are used to mark sacred sites and to summon the deities as well as to ask their blessing.

The symbolism of the feather is a compression, so to speak, of the bird. Humankind, seeing that birds can fly, has always been desirous of flight. The mythology of angels, airborne deities residing in heaven or heavens, is common to the collective human tribe. The wish to fly, understood on its primary level, is merely the desire to have something one does not or cannot have. On a deeper philosophical level, however, flight is the dreamlike movement of the unconscious, the freedom of will, the connection between the spiritual and the material. In flight, man releases his earthbound nature and is reborn in spirit.

The bird clan of the Chickasaw did not have to work. Like their namesake, they woke at first light and went to sleep at sundown. They were thought to be wise, independent, virtuous. Native American runners would often imitate birds in flight by running in units that were v-shaped. When the lead wind-breaker runner grew tired, the runner to his right filled the space as he dropped back; but the v formation of geese on the wing remained intact.

bluebird song

bluebird pollen we are blessed with
bluebird pollen we have feasted with
bluebird pollen touched our soul
bluebird spirit world we dwell in
bluebird song we sing
in the house of bird clan our life journeys
forever we shall make our life together
  in harmony

—From *Whimpering Chant* by Jay de Groat

FETISH

♦ ♦ ♦

The Portuguese word *feitico,* a noun, is defined as a "charm, sorcery, enchantment." In English, *fetish* as an adjective means "made by art, artificial, skillfully contrived." In Native American terms, the fetish was an object, large or small, that possessed consciousness, and therefore power.

However, Indian belief held that all things, whether animate or inanimate, possessed life. Plants, trees, stars, winds, herbs, rocks, and pollen are the embodiment of diverse beings and spirits. Such is the kingdom of the fetish, an object sought in dream, vision, thought, or action.

In a Zuni myth, monsters changed into stone contained within them the magic breath of their former life. These sacred stones, once owned by a man, were immediately transformed from negative to positive energy; thus, the fetish.

A fetish is acquired by a person, a family, or a people for the purpose of promoting welfare. It requires of its owner a mixture of reverence, prayer, and, sometimes, personal sacrifice. In time, if the owner of the fetish does not benefit by it, the object may lose its status and become a mere talisman. And it may fall lower in the owner's estimation and become only an ornament.

The fetish differs from what may be termed a guardian spirit because it can be bought, sold, loaned, or inherited. A guardian spirit, however, cannot be passed on.

Opposite: Beaded Plains Fetish.
I.A.I.A. Museum Collection.

Right: Taos Puebla Elk Fetish.
Courtesy W.E. Channing & Co.,
Santa Fe.

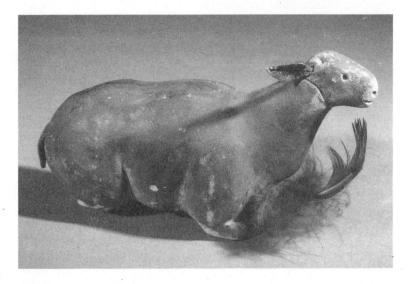

Taos Pueblo Buffalo Fetish.
Courtesy Rainbow Man, Santa Fe.
Photo: Bobbe Besold

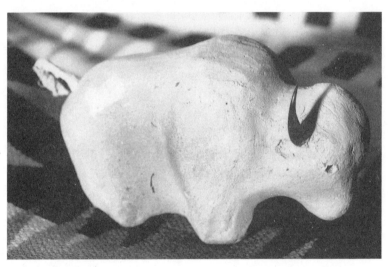

The fetish itself may be bone, feather, rock, wood, berry, even the skin of a lizard. It can come from a dream, be the gift of a medicine man, a trophy taken from a slain enemy, or an object of stone or wood resembling a bird, animal, or reptile. But whatever the fetish may look like, it must have—in the owner's mind—some symbolic connection with the power of the universe.

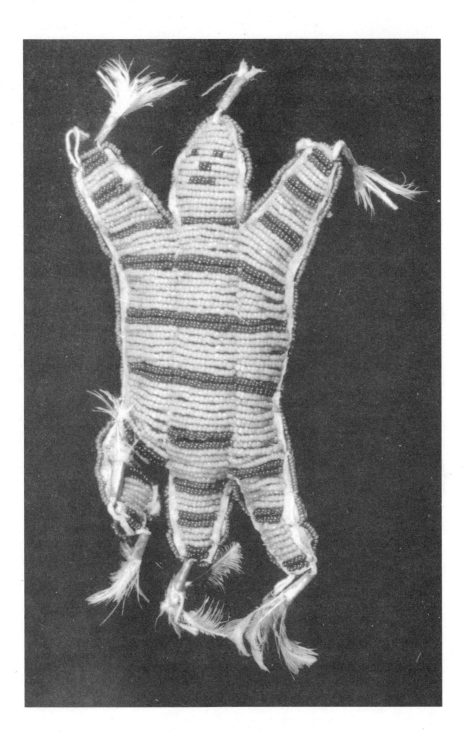

The placement of the fetish is yet another aspect of its universality. Some tribes fastened them to the scalp lock as a pendant; others hung them from the bridle of a horse or concealed them between the covers of a shield. The fetish could also be placed in a secret dwelling, tied to a child's cradle, worn on one's clothing, or placed in a sacred shrine. A certain Sioux fetish, the image of a man made out of stone, was placed in a cylindrical box filled with swan's down. A hunting and divining fetish of the Cherokee, a crystal, was wrapped in buckskin and kept in a secret cave where it was ritually fed the blood of a deer.

In most tribes, the mysterious origin of the fetish was personal medicine, the secret of its owner or maker, and this was revealed only to someone being initiated into its sacred use.

Some years ago, I found a small stone Madonna, which I showed to the writer Robert Boissiere. After examining it, he told me that it was almost identical to a Madonna (image of the Virgin of Guadalupe, the Amerindian patroness) he had found on Tiburón Island in the Sea of Cortez. He had been told by a Seri Indian friend that if he looked carefully, he would find his heart's desire (meaning his quest for truth) on the shore of that island. My own Madonna was discovered during a time of spiritual questioning, and was, in fact, the answer to a prayer of guidance. Today, both Madonnas, blessed with cornmeal, reside in a shrine deep within a kiva in northern New Mexico.

FISH

◆ ◆ ◆

one day
bear stops
to talk
with Singing River
wakes her
river with thousand-star eyes
rises to the
furry paws
she sings,
   "shhhh, whisper bear,
   my children are coming."

   —Loren Straight Eagle Plume

Cochiti Fish Design. Drawing by
Gaythner Gonzales.

Children of the river—the fish—were a source of food and inspiration to the American Indian. The spiritual essence of the fish
was that it could breathe in water—hence many myths involving
Hero Deities who were encharmed to do the same. As a supreme
member of the element of water, the fish was symbol of current,
flow, life activity from within the wetness of the earth. Like a bird,
it could fly through the water. But like a man, it seemed medita-
tive, a denizen of darkness as well as light, a slow and fast mover in
the streams, rivers, ponds, and lakes of Turtle Island:

In the clear current
Little trout imitate
The shadow
 of the heron.
Wind wrinkles
 the quiet pool.
The trout breathe,
 the deer drink.

Opposite: Harpooning. Photograph by Edward S. Curtis. Courtesy Rainbow Man, Santa Fe.

Above: Ready to Throw the Harpoon. Photograph by Edward S. Curtis. Courtesy Rainbow Man, Santa Fe.

In *Meditations with Animals,* there is a section on "Swimmer the Salmon," the name given by the Kwakiutl to the fish that returns to the river of its birth to spawn and then to die. This is not a riddle or a myth to the Kwakiutl but a picture of their own life, the roundness of it: fish returning year after year, the same way the spirit travels back into life after the severance of death. The endless round of living and dying:

> Now I am the swimmer who dies,
> who runs with rain and moon
> and salt-wind tide,
> river and falls
> and sweet pebble-water
> . . . Swimmer the Salmon
> who comes with the moon.

GAME

◆ ◆ ◆

At Jemez Pueblo
they catch a pebble
 with their toes

 Throw the pebble
with their foot

And so, run after it
 catch it
 kick it

In the cold snow
 in the cold
with a pebble
 catch-kick
And run
 in cold snow.

Native American games stem from ancient rituals derived from
the hunt. The tools of the game, if there are any, go back to the
bow and arrow. The concept of four quarters, four seasons, four
elements was the original form upon which the games were built.
When, after the passing of time, a ceremony gave way to a game,

Runners. Taos Pueblo.
Smithsonian Collection.

the game then survived as an amusement, but it maintained the tradition that inspired it.

Most Indian games came from curing and healing ceremonies, procreation or fertilization ceremonies, gaming-birthing-catching-hunting ceremonies.

The ball as a basic game tool was originally considered a sacred object that was not touched by the hand. Thus, the origin of soccer; it is now thought to have been developed by the Arawak Indians on the island of Jamaica. Naturally, the ball or sphere was identified with sun, moon, and earth.

Ring and pole games, of which there are many today, used a ring and a netted hoop: The net was the spiderweb, symbol of Mother Earth. The performance of this game was an enactment of an ancient fertility ceremony. Kicked-stick and ball-race games, the forerunners of American football, came from crop-protection

Plains Lacrosse Sticks. Courtesy W.E. Channing & Co., Santa Fe.

rituals that shielded gentle plants against windstorms. The boundaries were the four quarters into which the game (crop) was symbolically placed.

Native American hand games, such as hide-the-pea and stick-and-dice, originated with the Aztec. The game of tops, the universal child's spinning toy, was an indigenous game utilizing horn, bone, stone, or wood.

The snow snake game of the Iroquois, from which many American ice or snow sports have derived, was a winter fertility rite. The snake, a summer fertility symbol, was thrown along the frozen ground or upon the ice. The summer snake on the winter earth: a vision of spring.

Basketball, it has often been said, was a hoop game of American Indian origin played by Eastern tribes, and adopted by a white American teacher in Springfield, Massachusetts, at the turn of the century (1891).

Native American games have, at their heart, a form of spiritual training absent in most Americanized sports. They instill cooperation as well as competition, and, most important, obeisance. Something lacking in today's sporting events is the Native American willingness to learn from one's elders and to play for the spirit rather than the wallet. In Native American competitive running meets, elders urge, but do not force, youth to participate. The old way, the craft of the sport, is shared when the time is right, but more often it is learned through observance and practice rather than "coaching."

Steve Gachupin, Jemez pueblo champion runner and repeated winner of the Pike's Peak Marathon, once said, "When running, set your sights on the mountain, not the man in front of you."

HORSE

• • •

In Native American myths, the horse, came from the earth and the sun. History explains that it was given to the Indians by the Spanish conquerors, but the horse was long worshiped by the Aztecs before the coming of the Spanish. In fact, when the first Aztecs saw a man upon it, they viewed the two as one, and considered it a "magic being."

To the Dakota, the horse was *sunka wakan*, "the mysterious dog." The Shawnee called it *mishawa*, "elk." When Antonio de Espejo visited the Hopi in 1583, the Indians spread cotton scarves on the ground for his horses to walk upon.

Companion on the hunt, burden bearer, friend of the people, the horse became the literal backbone of the Plains tribes. In many of them, when a man died, his horse was killed so that it could take him to the next world. There is no question but that the horse mobilized the American Indian and created a new economy, based upon horse wealth. As a medium of exchange, the horse also became an incentive for tribal warfare. Foot-wandering tribes, once mounted, became fierce warriors—and also horse thieves.

The art of riding was something that the Indian took very seriously: to slide and ride around under a horse's neck, to become, as in the Aztec vision, one thing with the horse. Concealing themselves in battle while riding, mounting, and dismounting with deft skill, tribal people regarded these forms of discipline as a pleasure, and it was obvious they surpassed their white foes in the art.

A cavalry officer once met a Plains chief to discuss a treaty: The two parties met on horseback. The white men, following the precise format of dressage, came on in rows of well-uniformed soldiers. The chief, seeing this and thinking it quite elementary, sent his warriors out into a revolving pattern of concentric circles that baffled the cavalry with its dizzying complexity.

The Plains tribes practiced horse dances; they sang songs and prayers about horses and they had horse games. In the dances of the horse-soldier societies, the men rode during the dance. Also, the horses were painted, tails tied up as in preparation for war. Hawk or owl feathers were tied to forelock or tail. Sometimes a human scalp hung from the horse's lower jaw. The painted print of a hand on either side of the neck indicated an enemy on foot had been ridden down.

Before battle, horses were rubbed and "blown upon" with medicine to ensure invincibility. Among certain Plains tribes, horse doctors were devoted to healing and protecting horses just as veterinarians are today. These doctors aided horses injured on the battlefield and in the hunt, and they were always called upon before and after intertribal horse races, which were popular among the tribes.

According to Spanish Barb horse breeder Olivia Tsosie:

What is important for the reader to understand is that Indian horse culture, particularly in the Great Plains, had no stables, no corrals, no grain, no horse blankets, and little metal. Like the Spanish, the Indians mounted from the "off" side, used rawhide ropes, reins, picketing and hobbling lines, and "bridles." Metal was so rare that the whole array of tack we are familiar with was replicated with wood, hide, and thongs.

Appaloosas on the Run. Drawing by Mariah Fox.

Imagine that one had to maintain one's herds by active, 24-hour herding activities, lest they disappear over the horizon. Imagine that one would picket one's well-trained horses next to the tipi—with the picket stake serving as a tent peg, so that if the horse pulled it out, one would know it. Imagine taming a horse taken from the herd by roping, what magic one might invoke to bind the horse forever, breathing on it, receiving its breath, and learning to know what it would do, as well as how to get it to do what one wanted. A horse can be guided with a stick tapping its shoulder, the pressure of legs, or the connection with a bit or bosal. The Indians used all of these techniques. Lacking the Christian concept of Adam as the dominator of all nature, the Indian would not have used domination as the goal of interaction with horses.

Among the many horse songs or prayers, some of the most beautiful are from the Navajo:

I am the Sun's son.
I sit upon a turquoise horse
At the opening of the sky.

This is Elder Brother, the masculine Hero Twin, speaking. The equation of mystic power comes from the Sun Father (his own real father), the horse of turquoise (a real horse that dances in the clouds with a rainbow in its mouth for a bridle), and the region of the sky (itself a father, a masculine symbol). The song celebrates horse, deity, and man, all at the same time. It goes on to sing that such a magnificent thing as the turquoise horse must belong to all the people, not just to a solitary rider.

In the Navajo "Song of the Horse," all aspects of the animal are celebrated—his neigh, the dust of his hooves, the fresh flowers he feeds upon, the holy waters he drinks, and the mist of pollen in which he is hidden.

Mysterious dog, elk, deity that treads on clouds . . .

Once, in a remote place called Horse Creek Canyon, not far from where I make my home in Tesuque, New Mexico, I found a wreckage of bleached white horse bones:

> And it was as if,
> Standing live and whole, the horse had been
>   bowled
> By a giant, broken into shards. For a mile up canyon
>   you could
> Count the bones, each piece a sand-polished gemstone
> The flute-shaped neck, swan-like and firm
> Pretty in its bed of mica schist.

> Once this horse
>   stood proud
> Mane in the wind, moon in the eye. I think: better to
> Have been a horse than a man: wandering the back canyons
> Until time should break you down to bits of bone.

I take the jawbone
Home, mount it in a window—
So those mad proud teeth can bite the moon
  sing the song
Of Horse Creek Canyon.

Navajo Horse Race. Photo Number UN 24. 01. Museum of Indian Arts and Culture/Laboratory of Anthropology, Santa Fe.

HOUSE

◆ ◆ ◆

The concept of the Native American dwelling was that it should conform to the contours of Mother Earth. The Navajo prayer goes as follows:

House made of winds
House made of fur
House made of pollens
House made of flint
House made of crystals . . .

And thus all the houses of the deities are given their due, and, lastly, the house of man:

Bless my house made of mud
Resin and pine.
Bless my family made of blood
Marrow and bone.

Houses, temporary or permanent, were centered around ceremonial values: The cutting and sewing of a tepee cover was attended with ritual exactitude. The Navajo hogan always faces east, in keeping with the rising sun. American Indian houses were usually round or half-round, dome-shaped or oval. Often they were hol-

Navajo Hogan. Photograph by Edward S. Curtis. Courtesy Rainbow Man, Santa Fe.

lowed out of the earth. Without square or plumb line, these dwellings were beautiful, simple, and durable. They did not take more space than was necessary. Made of natural materials, Indian houses were ecologically sound, often designed to be carried away or left to dissolve back into the earth. Such words as *wickiup, tepee, igloo, wigwam,* and *hogan* are common to most Americans, and the ritual of camping in America owes much to them.

The large communal dwellings of the Indians, the ones known as longhouses of the Iroquois, were fifty to one hundred feet long and sixteen to eighteen feet wide. Constructed of frame poles, bark siding, and a triangular-shaped roof, the longhouses were divided inside into various compartments, with a central smoke hole in the roof. The Mandan communal house was circular, about forty feet in diameter, supported by a series of posts and crossbeams. The wide roof and sloping sides were covered with willow or brush matting and earth.

Perhaps the most successful of all communal dwellings in

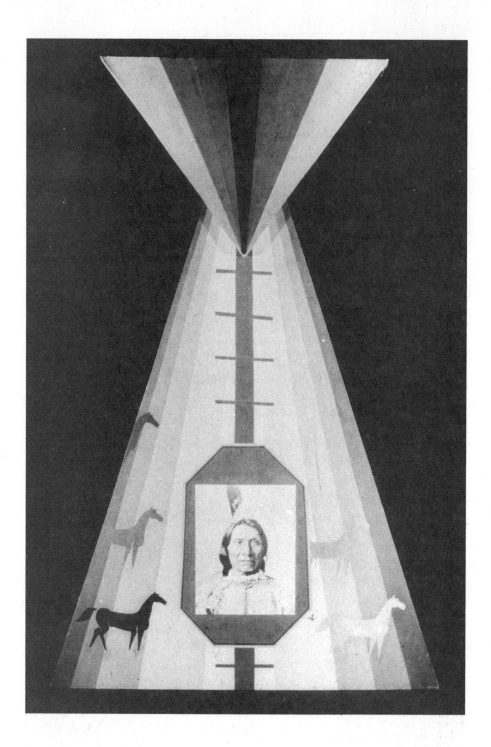

Native America are the pueblos, which are still inhabited today. Many-celled clusters of stone or adobe brick were built into what might be termed the first apartment house in North America. Those built in prehistoric times were semicircular; the others, as you see them today in northern New Mexico and Arizona, are built around a central court or plaza.

Built in terrace form, the lower section of the pueblo had a one-story tier of apartments. The next section had two stories. The next tier sometimes added up to seven stories. The masonry was usually small, flat stones laid into adobe mortar. Sometimes balls of adobe were used as building stones, or a double row of wattling was filled in with solidly tamped grout. Walls of this kind were sometimes five to seven feet thick. The hivelike structure of the pueblo made it safe and strong and ideal for communal living.

Single-family dwellings of the Paiute and Cocopah consisted of brush shelters for summer. Winter dwellings were made of poles bent together at the top and covered with brush, bark, and earth. In prehistoric and early historic times, in the Ohio valley and the valley of the Mississippi, the Indians made circular wigwams of bark built over a shallow excavation.

The Plains Indian tepee, as used by the Sioux, Arapaho, Comanche, and Kiowa, was of the portable-tent variety. However, the tepees of the Omaha and Osage were more substantial. They placed posts together in a circle, bound them with willows, and backed them with dried grass. The entire structure was then covered with well-packed "sods."

In the Navajo song of White Corn Boy, the roundness of life, the shape of the hogan, and the intent to live a life of harmony are intermixed:

White Corn Boy

I walk on the straight path that is towards my home.
I walk to the entrance of my home.

I arrive at the beautiful goods curtain which hangs at the
  doorway.
I arrive at the entrance of my home.
I am in the middle of my home.
I am at the back of my home. . . .

Before me it is beautiful,
Behind me it is beautiful,
Under me it is beautiful,
Above me it is beautiful,
All around me it is beautiful.

INDIAN

• • •

Frank Waters writes in *Masked Gods: Navajo and Pueblo Ceremonialism:*

> If there exists such a thing as a spirit-of-place, imbuing each of the continental land masses of the world with its own unique and ineradicable sense of rhythm, mood, and character, and if there exists an indigenous form of faith deriving from it, then it is to the Indian we must look for that expression of life's meaning which alone differentiates America from Europe, Africa and Asia.

Ute-Comanche Peace Treaty Signing 1977. Jim Bay Spirit Horse, Ute. I.A.I.A. Museum Collection.

Yes—but what is America if not a classic error in geographic misappropriation? What is Indian if not a compound error based on the same erroneous proposition?

Christopher Columbus, as we now all seem to be aware, miscalculated his presence in the Caribbean by thinking that he had arrived in the waters of *Cipangu,* or Japan. In attempting to find a new route to the Indies of the East, he mistakenly wound up in the Indies of the West. The people with whom he lived in 1493, on his second voyage from Spain, were Arawak "Indians" from South America, tribal people who had drifted into the islands in or about the early 1300s, fleeing the fierce cannibalistic Caribs. The Arawak

Navajo Horseman. Photo Number 70.1/2576. Adelaide Law Collection, Museum of Indian Arts and Culture/Laboratory of Anthropology, Santa Fe.

are the people Columbus called Indians. The rest is history—or what we call history. Actually, it is error.

The Arawaks kept barkless dogs, grew and smoked their own tobacco, played football (soccer), and slept in an invention all their own—the hammock. They talked to Columbus about a furious god that frequently visited them, known as Hurricane, and they were very friendly. Ultimately, this was their undoing. One hundred years after the Columbus discovery, there were fewer than five hundred Arawaks left in the islands. By the seventeenth century, they were—to use the Indian word—*heeleewawa* (gone).

The name Indian first occurs in a letter from Columbus dated February 1493. The explorer speaks of *Indios*. One can only guess from engravings what the original encounter must have been like, but the Arawaks were trusting enough to travel off to Europe with their white overlords, to discover sickness and death at the hands of people who found them merely a curiosity.

In succeeding centuries, the term *Indian* became fixed, often "aided" by the adjective *red* to describe a skin color that was more accurately a brownish hue. In the nineteenth century, the term *redskin* as a derogatory reference was popular, stemming perhaps from the French *peau-rouge. Indian,* slurred and damaged by prejudice, became *Injun.* As Loren Straight Eagle Plume explains, it is not easy to carry the names, the visions, the wishes, lies, and fantasies the white world has put upon the Indian:

Wish to Walk Thru Walls

Mr. Longhair
Mr. Highcheekbones
Mr. Peyotebreath

When I dream
   I see a thousand
      a thousand feather-crowned warriors
They are silhouetted
   by an old Sun of seasons long gone
The moment I cannot picture them in my mind
 is the moment I begin to decay

     These warrior's mouths
     dry, lips rough with
      dust of forgotten miles

I can't find the anger that once
 powered my innocent thoughts

Purity is only a memory

Then why, why can't I think thoughts
   I thought just a moment ago
Think about that thought
   I thought
     can't I think
Then why,
Think about
      just a moment ago
   I thought
       and things fell apart . . .

     So, lacking the ability
      to walk through walls
       I sit here
       in class

     —Loren Straight Eagle Plume

Of course, the inheritors of the names did not call themselves
anything but The People. In referring to tribes outside their own
parameters, designations of place were common, such as The
People of the Red Willow, or The People of the Salty Marsh.

In Canada, the colonial term was *sauvage,* which, however, does
not translate literally into "savage." The historian Bernard De Voto
has speculated that had the French fully colonized America, the
relationship between the races might have been different.
Certainly the French approach in the New World, with regard to
Indian people, was closer to synchronicity. In many ways, the
French trapper and explorer, in his willingness to adopt Indian

ways, became a kind of white Indian. More than other Europeans, the French learned Indian languages and engaged in open inter-marriage. In contrast, the Spanish approach was a kind of conquest by dominance, which did not actually forbid marriage but did not promote it either.

It was the emerging nation of Americans, though, who set out to "get the land" any way they could, prohibitive of marriage. The Indian, in their eyes, was strictly an inferior. Thus, the white man in America became a universal enemy—a person of one skin to the Native American.

On the gazetteer records and maps of long ago, the adjective Indian preceded every noun describing every conceivable spot of land. This was obviously because the whole continent was an Indian place—not Indian-owned but Indian-inhabited.

Here were places where no white person had ever set foot. So, on the early maps, each location bore the rightful Indian first name:

bay, bayou, beach, bottom, branch, brook
camp, cove, creek, cross
dig, draft
fall, field, ford
gap, grove, gulch
harbour, head, hill

heeleewawa

JUNIPER

◆ ◆ ◆

Native Americans chewed juniper berries to ward off contagious diseases such as scarlet fever, smallpox, and typhus. Six to ten berries each day were recommended, the taste being pleasant and good for digestion. In addition, berries were chewed to cure coughing, shortness of breath, cramps, and convulsions. In medicine ceremonies, still performed today, the burning bough of juniper is used to keep the mind awake and clear. The Navajo place green juniper needles in a pan and burn them until only the ash remains, this they mix with water, and then strain. The resultant liquid is a mordant.

Juniper Branch. Drawing by Mariah Fox.

In the landscape of the Four Corners country, the area where Utah, Arizona, New Mexico, and Colorado touch corners, the earth sings a special song. Some say it is the light, the etheric blue, acetylene blue, turquoise blue sky. Others claim it is the earth, the way it has soaked sun and rain, fire and snow for so many millions of years, because it has been the parched skin of the immemorial Mother for so long, now one can trace, in the scarlines of the millennia, the suffering she has borne . . . and yet, she is ever-resilient.

And it is the scent and sight of cedar, the sacred tree of the high desert. You smell it coming into the pueblo on a starlit night. In ceremonies of the kiva, cedar smoke is a blessing; its fragrance is in the sweat lodge and on the winter clothes of men cutting wood and stacking it in front of their mud houses. Talking God of the

Navajo, the maternal grandfather of all the deities, appears in the dance with his head mask of buckskin, his cornstalk nose, a circlet of spruce decorating his shoulders.

Cedar, warped by the wind of centuries. Bent, hunched into the shape of a crone, an eerie chanting old woman of the rain-wind-snow-sun. From the bitter earth, the fruited earth comes this tree that was young when Jesus of Nazareth gave away loaves and fishes, and now, ever-green, is old with the passing of time.

Green is the symbol of everlasting life. The sprig of green, the whir of rattle, the *shush-shush* of ankle bells, the lift and stamp of feet, these are the old ways, the incontrovertible pattern in the ancient grain of wood:

> The way the bark looks, wind-peeled and gnarled
> like a woman
> Wetted in the rain.
> Saw the wood in hot summer, throw it in the chunk
> Pile for the cold winter to come. The red, dead
> Juniper dust carries the pungent scent of
> Red chili; sweet dust reminds as it floats into
> the face: San Ildefonso Pueblo.
> Warm in woolen blankets, winter bells of dancers
> and the chili by firelight after.
> Water juniper—she drinks just once in a while—
> The loving wood
> that warms us: once, when we cut
> twice, when we burn
>   three times
> When we smell the smoke and remember summer in the
> sweet grain.

KIVA

◆ ◆ ◆

The great kiva at Chetro Ketl in Chaco Canyon, the broken
    slabstone walls of the pueblo ruin and massive walls of
    the sandstone cliff behind it,

A huge circular pit dug deep in the rocky ground, lined with
    slab and block stones, altars of heavier stones set inward, disks
    for pillar support set in stone wells,

Excavated by our best archaeologists, left roofless exposed to
    whatever interpretation you wish to impute to it, the
    mystery of it haunts you, the primitive feeling of it,
    meaning of it.

Say it represents the womb of earth, the cave of darkness from
    which man emerged into the light, sipapu the outlet, say it
    contained the beliefs, the cosmology of a vanished people.

—From *The Great Kiva* by Phillips Kloss

The kiva, a sacred ceremonial chamber, still used by the Pueblo
people is, in addition to its religious function, an accurate symbol
for the geophysical world. It is expressive of the four elements
because it embodies the characteristics of each. For instance, the

Ancient Ceremonial Kiva at
Bandelier National Monument,
New Mexico. Photograph by Joe
Hedrick.

kiva, residing under the ground like a cave, is representative of
Mother Earth. Within its round walls, there is the eternally lit fire,
which naturally draws its life from the air around it. The water jar
symbolizes the water element. Earth, air, fire, and water—the pri-
mordial components of life as we know it.

In the four worlds, or geophysical planes of this earth, we can
also trace a definite correspondence to Pueblo cosmography. First
the earth was a roiling ball of fire, then, cooled by the spuming
seas, it was frozen into rock and, finally, made into earth. Aided by
oxygen, the earth permitted life-forms to live upon it. This scien-
tific genesis of planet earth is also a template for the Pueblo
mythos of the birth of The People, who, groping in darkness,

inhabited all of the early developmental stages of inchoate life.

But this is not all: The kiva embodies much more. To begin again, on a religious or philosophical plane, fire, the first element, is, to the Indian, power, procreative and destructive.

Air or wind is the breath of life, or that which gives it continuance. It is carrier and restorer, informer and healer. Of course, it can also be a destroyer.

Water is all that liquid would be: blood, sweat, and tears, as well as urine and sperm. The waterway is another carrier. It is, in the myths, the birther into the next world. It is also the separator and joiner of the sexes. Water, too, can be destructive, and its ways must be known and understood.

Earth is the fruitful source of all life. Bountiful, feminine, the sponsor of harmony and order, earth is the mother of all, the Earth Mother. As water may be seen symbolically as blood, so then is the earth viewed as flesh.

Through kiva initiations, human beings become one with the nature of the universe. The unfolding of consecutive and consonant worlds is also a part of the human experience on a daily level. In the kiva, the ages of man and earth are reunited to form a symbiosis. The kiva, a living universe, is the great teacher of past, present, and future:

Deep in the dream kiva
  we slept through the winter
with woodsmoke in our hair.
  Rose from that dark
feathered warmth, in the spring,
  to make the new corn lean
on the long summer moon.

LAND

◆ ◆ ◆

*Looking Toward the Lawrence
Ranch, 1930s.* Courtesy Roy
Wright.

Once, a long time ago, before the arrival of the white man to the
land called Turtle Island, there were Indian-named places and
pathways that still had the freshness of birth upon them. The
Appalachian tribes named them in this way:

> great salted standing water
> where the sun shines out
> at the bushy place
> at the place of mud
> first or oldest planted ground
> the dancing place
> at the pine spring
> a long straight river
> a meadow
> bull thistle
> tidewater covered with froth
> the place where clams are found
> the sprucy stream
> at the sweating place
> at the sweet land
> the place of fear
> the place where deer are shy
>   —From *Apalache* by Paul Metcalf

Looking Toward the Lawrence Ranch, 1930s. Courtesy Roy Wright.

In none of the previous text do we find a hint of ownership. The places were young and innocent and almost absent of designation. To the Native American, *land* is Mother Earth.

A mother, by definition, is one who gives birth to and cares for her children. Thus, the Indian concept of the nurturing source of all good comes from within, not from without, the fecundity of maternal earth. This is a spiritual rather than a material relationship to land. The idea is far removed from the white European notion of land being something to give tenure to, something to own, something from which to reap benefit.

Furthermore, the Native American Earth Mother value system was a great deal more than that: It was religion. Property and self-aggrandizement, that which arises from ownership of land, was a desecration of Indian religion. You do not take from the Mother; she gives freely to those whose reverence is declared by familial responsibility: sonhood and daughterhood are rewarded with nourishment and love. (The same familial, tribal union exists in the Hebrew translation of the Old Testament of the Bible. Yahweh rewards those to whom the sacrifice of love and obedience is innate and unpremeditated. In this sense, even though Yahweh is a

Navajo Reservation, Monument Valley. Photograph by Joe Hedrick.

symbol of fatherhood, he shows a dual nature, a mothering tendency, and acts as both mother and father to his children.)

Mother, being impartial, could not offer her blessing to one of her children and not to another (this differs in large measure with the Old Testament Yahweh). Therefore, the Native American Earth Mother would not allow her flesh, the land itself, to be appropriated by one individual or tribe, to the exclusion of any other(s). All must benefit—or none. This was the way it was, and still is.

This idea of impartial motherhood was once explained to me by a Navajo friend, Ray Brown, who said that though the Sun Father was a powerful deity, his very power and strength could overwhelm (Yahweh destroying the cities of Sodom and Gomorrah) Earth Surface People. Yet not so with Mother Earth. The Sun Father might burn a man with all-powerful rays, and Changing Woman, the Earth Mother, with the proper herbs, would heal the burn and make it well again. Always, the Mother restrains and protects her offspring, birthing and helping and healing.

The attitude of sharing the goodness of Mother Earth is opposed to the selfish individuation of land tenure, which may be defined as a secular tending of the earth. Instead of depending on the outflow of mother's milk, so to speak, man, uncertain of mother's love, takes control of the soil and works it his way. In doing so, he becomes an occupant of the area he tends and the place from which he derives food is his dependency, his place of tenure. Although the Pueblo Indians of the Southwest, in particular, "tended" the land, they also worshiped it. Their tending was not separate from their obeisance, their attitude of reverence. The harvest dance and the harvest itself are not apart from one another; they are joined. Even the Badlands, in their bitter beauty, are sacred ground:

Bisti

    the badlands become magical
    in the morning air
    come back to me

Northwest New Mexico
    well known by the Jicarilla Apache and the Navajo

    distinctly bitter
    in the mid-day dry
    come back to me

nothing straight about it
    except striations appear in the sedimentary formations
they color horizontal stripes
    tan, grey, black, hit strikingly
they make the landscape move

religious sky
in dusk's light
come back to me

Bisti's formations, in the high desert
are cloaked figures, gathered for a ritual

—Loren Straight Eagle Plume

Frank Hamilton Cushing, the great observer of the Zuni people,
said that a Zuni man might farm a field of unclaimed land, and it
would then belong to him. However, in truth, it was considered
the property of his clan. Upon his death, the land might be cultivated by any member of his clan (but not by his wife or children,
who must be of another clan). Indians of other tribes in North
America often fought among themselves over desirable territory,
such as hunting and fishing grounds. While dealing in occupancy,
however, they did not consider land as merchantable; instead it
was seen as life-sustainable.

In recent times, the conflict of land as merchandise and land as
mother came up in the 1930s. John Steinbeck's *The Grapes of
Wrath* is a biblical treatise of white society in modern America:
land ownership versus land nurtureship. When Rose of Sharon
offers her breast to the old man and saves his life with her mother's milk, the point is clearly made. Those who care for the earth
also care for one another. The sharing is unilateral. This is a clear
and definite Native American, earth-worship, tribal value system.

In 1783, the Continental Congress forbade private purchase or
acceptance of lands from Indians. On the adoption of the
Constitution, the right of eminent domain became vested in the
United States, and Congress alone had the power to extinguish the
Indians' right of occupancy.

In 1887, 104 years later, the Dawes Act provided that every Native
American was to be given "a piece of reservation." The surplus

Navajo Lookout. Photograph by
Joe Hedrick.

land, that which was left over, was purchasable by the United
States government for $1.25 per acre. In 1933, forty-six years later,
Indian-owned land had dwindled from 138 million to 52 million
acres.

In 1865, the Duwamish chief Sealth, speaking of land ownership,
said something that has often been quoted. It seems to contain the
very atom of disagreement between the two anatomically different
cultures, Indian and white:

How can you buy or sell the sky—the warmth of the land?
The idea is strange to us. We do not own the freshness of the air
or the sparkle of the water. How can you buy them from us? . . .

We know that the white man does not understand our way. One portion of the land is the same to him as the next, for he is a stranger who comes in the night and takes from the land whatever he needs . . . .

In 1978, I received a gift from an elderly Pueblo potter from Santa Clara. When she gave the pot to me, she also gave me a Polaroid snapshot of herself. The two she said were one. The pot and the potter were not separate, nor was the clay from which the pot came. All of these, she said, came out of the earth:

> I sit on a black plastic chair
> and my hands hold
> the round earth waterjar
> my ancestors made.
>
> The water is gone
> from the jar, broken.
>
> I hold on to the jar
> because it is made
> of the earth mother.
>
> I am the jar.

Jay de Groat expresses the pottery bowl as "a vessel of harmony in holy matrimony":

> *Potlatch*
>
> around the lip
> the rainbow lay horizontally
> in the direction the sun journeys

there are absences of motifs
only scars of its use
through three generations

a vessel of harmony in holy matrimony
a tympanum of songs in spiritual communion
a bowl of herbs in healing ceremony
a kettle of corn in sustaining life

the essences of clay in the earthen ware
comes from the hollow of its vacancy
just as we endure what is not
and to use what is

LION

• • •

In Incan cosmology, there was an inner earth, the moon house, in which was enclosed a puma; the bird-tailed puma leaped over the sun—always the puma and the condor, intertwined. Carvings in stone depict llama, puma, fish, cougar, condor; earth, sun, moon, sky. Andean man saw the sun-animal, atop the world, sun lord, his deity, the puma, nibbling the moon, from full to crescent and letting it grow again.

A ritual song of the Osage also depicts the male power of the puma:

> I am the male puma who lies
> upon the earth.
> I am a person who had made a
> male puma of his body.
> The knowledge of my courage
> has spread over the land.
> The god of day sits in the heavens.
> I sit close to the god of day.
> When men make me their god,
> all deaths die
> as they travel the paths of life.

Puma. Robert Gordon Mare.
Courtesy Sunstone Press.

Thus the poor panther, creature of godlike dimension to the
Andean Incan and the American Indian, was declared an arch
enemy of man by the European settlers who came to Turtle Island.

The word *puma* seems to have come from an Incan word, while
cougar, meaning the same thing, came from a corruption of an
Amazonian Indian word. In the Rocky Mountains, the Americans

called them mountain lions; in the South and East, panthers.

Today, partly because of the myth of ferocity (like the wolf), there are but a handful of these noble, spirited, little-known members of the animal world. Nature writer Edward Hoagland speculated that in the 1970s, there were "four to six thousand left in the United States."

What happened to the elusive mountain lion, the panther of myth, the deity of the American Indian? The cryptic, unsociable animal had to go deeper and deeper into the upland canyon and lowland swamp if it wanted to survive. However, curiosity got the cat: As secretive as it always was, and is, it never seemed to learn the lesson that man did not want it around. Perhaps it had gotten used to its divinity status among the tribes, and could not figure the white man out. In any case, though, cat attacks have been few and far between. "In this century in the United States," according to Hoagland, "only one person, a child of thirteen, has been killed by a mountain lion; that was in 1924." The animal, as predator, was too fearsome a prospect to have around. The myth of the animal's cunning and devious nature, its scary hiss and yowl, its preference for darkness, and its predilection for meat, all have led to its not-so-gradual demise.

The Indian revered the cat, calling it the "soft-footed brother." As with all animals in the natural world, Native Americans saw a purpose that grafted the lion to the man. The huntsman and the tracker saw in the secretive cat a mirror reflection, and in its golden hide there was the intimation of immortality. It was thought among some tribes that the flesh of the cougar would ensure immortality. At the least, it was believed that because of the creature's sun symbolism, it was a near relation, if not a direct symbol of, the Sun Father. The animal's sense of pride, of knowing its place and not deviating from it, placed it at the top of the animal pantheon, but also at a level with people.

Despite its reputation for ferocity, the mountain lion is known to quit in struggles that ultimately decide its fate. Somehow magnetized by human beings, paths always crossing, the curious cat would rather scavenge than brawl. Mortified by humans with dogs who chased after it, the mountain lion often merely submitted to the terrors of the rope—mountain lion roping being a sport of the last century—by allowing itself to be pulled from the tree to a groveling death by dog, bullet, or strangulation.

What is there about the divine that brought out the profane in the American—that still brings it out? For the great cat is no better off now, museum- and zoo-bound, than in the last quarter of the century. And as we rapidly, fiendishly, seek to protect it, we are expertly killing off its place of refuge.

As D. H. Lawrence said upon finding a hunted-down, dead mountain lion in the mountains of Questa, New Mexico:

> And I think in this empty world there was room
> for me and a mountain lion.
> And I think in the world beyond, how easily we might
> spare a million or two humans
> And never miss them.
> Yet what a gap in the world, the missing white frost-
> face of that slim yellow mountain lion!

MASK

• • •

Opposite: Mask of Octupus Hunter—Qagyuhl (Kwakiutl). Photograph by Edward S. Curtis. Courtesy Rainbow Man, Santa Fe.

Many tribes held the belief that in the beginning of time (in the time of beginnings), all animated beings had a dual existence. A man had the power to become, at will, either his human or his animal self. So, too, an animal could reveal the face and form of his human self. Thus were man and animal one; thus were man and animal two: dual creatures in a unified world.

On a vision quest, an ordinary Indian man might be permitted to see into his animal nature, his animal self. He might also peer into the face of a creature, a bird perhaps, and see its feathers part to reveal the "manface" hidden inside.

A tribal mask was designed to give the wearer power. The making of a mask, therefore, had to be done in ceremonial fashion. The poem below is a retelling from the Navajo:

Find the hide of a deer not killed by a weapon;
Draw the cutting lines for the skin with a crystal.
 Use the sinew from the right side of the spinal column
For sewing the right side of the head-dress.

Yellow feathers from the little yellow bird are sewn on
 the right side and the work is done by a right-handed
man.

For the left side, use the sinew from that side of the
  spinal column.
  A left-handed man must sew bluebird feathers
On the left side of the head-dress.

The right side feathers are for the black water jar
  which brings rain.
The left side feathers are for the ears of corn.
The dancer with the head-dress, the mask, is called
  Cornfather.

Sacred masks of the Hopi were put on and off only with the left hand. In addition, bodily purification accompanied the painting of a mask. Hopi masks are made of leather, cloth, and basketry; they are also adorned with wood, bark, hair, woven fabric, feathers, herbs, and bits of gourd.

Thunderbird masks of some of the Siouan tribes were made by boys when thunder was first heard talking in the spring. After the masks were made, the boys then visited their uncles' tepees. There they made the sound of thunder by striking the tepee flaps with sticks. Once they were invited inside, the mask wearers were given presents of leggings, moccasins, or blankets.

In general, the Native American mask is a symbol of animal/human/deity revelation and affirmation:

The painted mask he wore was in the dance, the lifting
  of his feet
The putting down of his weight: firm, soft, strong, sure.
The dust
Came up in clouds of gold and his face was hidden there in
  evergreen, feather, rose-gold dust and clay paint, white
  and black.
When his eyes met mine, they started, were startled, just

Qagyuh (Kwakiutl) Mask.
Photograph by Edward S. Curtis.
Courtesy Rainbow Man, Santa Fe.

As the deer quakes before the hunter when it is first seen
 and sees.

In that second's glance the hunter knows if the deer is his
 or whether it is not, and if not, and must then go free.
He looked at me
 through the mask of a thousand or more years, and though I
 thought myself the hunter and he the deer, he went free
And I stayed tied to that spot until the dance was
 ended.

MEDICINE

❖ ❖ ❖

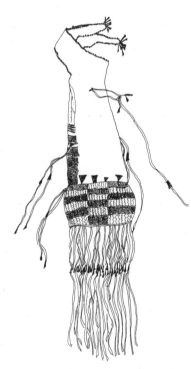

Sioux Beaded Buckskin Tobacco Pouch. Drawing by Mariah Fox.

Among some Native American tribes, the word *medicine* is synonymous with the word *mystery*. And so, a medicine man is a mystery man. Generally speaking, medicine in Indian culture means two things: plant, vegetal, herbal cures; and what we might call, for lack of a better term, psychic healing. Often the two are used simultaneously and interchangeably by the same practitioner. They are also used separately, with different practitioners, however.

Herbal healing uses plants, roots, twigs, and bark. Usually, a single plant is used, but it is also common to use as many as four. In Jamaica, an herbal practice passed down from the Arawak to the Ashanti involves the use of two plants, never one, as a curative. Animal and mineral medicine are also quite common in Native American healing. The Papago use crickets as medicine; the Tarahumara, lizards; and the Apache, spiders' eggs. The Navajo apply red ocher mixed with fat against sunburn. The barren, red clay from under the camp fire is used by the White Mountain Apache to induce sterility. The Hopi use blown ash on the skin to counteract a burn. Often, the thing that caused the infection or disease is the cure. For example, the Navajo apply the ash of the centipede on the sting itself to draw out the poison. The ventral surface of a poisonous snake is applied by many Southwestern tribes to the bite of the same snake.

The nature of disease in Native American definition is as much psychic as physical. It was, in fact, the belief in "offended deities" or sorcerers that gave the medicine man or woman a position of importance in Indian society. In Navajo terms, sickness is a falling out of harmony, a dis-ease with oneself brought on by advertent or inadvertent actions. The Navajo medicine man or woman may use a combination of emetic, prayer, song, dance, and sand painting to effect a cure.

Medicine people were recognized as having special gifts—innate and untrained—and also a sense of remedial knowledge passed down to them. Geronimo, an Apache shaman, was gifted from birth in the art of making medicine. Subject to visions and able to make chants that helped his people escape from enemies, he was a powerful medicine man. Among the Dakota, there were two kinds of medicine people: *wakan witshasha,* "mystery man"; and *pejihuta witshasha,* "grass-root man." In Jamaica, the Arawak/African medicine man was given the name bush doctor; the practitioner of white magic or supernatural power was given the name myal man (or woman).

The mystery man, whose power was of the psychic kind, obtained his gifts usually through dreams, vision quests. Often his gifts were merely given to him before birth. Hand-tremblers, who are Navajo diagnosticians, are of the "given type." Stargazers, also diagnosticians, are instructed through apprenticeship.

In most tribes, the so-called psychic medicine man was perhaps feared as well as respected, since he enjoined the functions of priest and shaman as well as healer. His word, thought, and influence were strong in the tribe. Medicine women of this kind are present in the Apache and Navajo tribes, as well as in certain others. Mostly, though, the herbalists (nonpsychic medicine people) were women. Among some tribes, there were, and are, medicine societies wherein the principal members are patients who have been cured of serious ailments. In addition to participating in their own ceremonies, these survivors are also called upon to assist the medicine people.

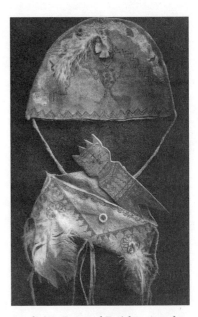

Medicine Cap and Fetish—Apache. Photograph by Edward S. Curtis. Courtesy Rainbow Man, Santa Fe.

Untitled. Don Whitesinger
(Navajo). I.A.I.A. Museum
Collection.

The Medicine Man of Jemez

"I will show you some medicine," said the elder.
But all night while we waited, he did nothing
  but smile a thin birdlike smile.
Finally, when it was time to leave and we started
  for the door, he handed John a conch shell.
"Blow this," he commanded.

John did as he was told: a mellow tone as of the
  sea-god, Neptune, arose in the still desert
  air of the quiet pueblo.
Red in the face, out of air, John faded on the
  conch.
"Again," the medicine man said, "louder."
John blew louder: the note went out farther into
  the night, touched the softest stars, made
  them giggle like children.
The old man medicine man smiled, went on smiling.
  And something
  was revealed.

MOCCASIN

◆ ◆ ◆

Cheyenne Footwear. Photograph by Edward S. Curtis. Courtesy Rainbow Man, Santa Fe.

With the exception of the sandal-weaving tribes living near or along the boundaries of Mexico (and certain tribes who traditionally went barefoot), most Native Americans wore a soft skin shoe known as a moccasin. The word probably came from one of the eastern Algonquin dialects and is spelled variously: *mocussin* in Narrangansett; *m'cusun* in Micmac; and *makisin* in Chippewa.

There were two primary types of moccasins: those with a rawhide sole sewed to a leather upper, and those with a sole and upper consisting of one piece of soft leather with a seam at the instep and heel. The former belongs to the eastern, or "timber," tribes and the latter to the western, or Plains, tribes. The boot or legging moccasin, worn from Alaska to Arizona, is still a part of the traditional woman's costume among the Pueblo people. The men also commonly wear what is known today as the "squaw boot" or "Taos Moccasin"—an elk- or rawhide-soled desert boot with a concho on the side. The legging portion of the Pueblo woman's moccasin and the man's squaw boot was once made of hand-tanned deerskin. Today, it is made of soft cowhide.

To an Indian of a former century, the moccasin represented utility and artistry at the same time. Elaborate quillwork or bead-work usually decorated the facing or front of the moccasin. In principle, the moccasin was a practical way of covering the foot,

while at the same time muffling its sound. It permitted the wearer to tread softly through the forest or upon snow or sand. Lightweight and allowing maximum foot movement, the moccasin is a practical, lovely, simple piece of universal footwear.

Woodland Beaded Moccasins. I.A.I.A. Museum Collection.

MUSIC

• • •

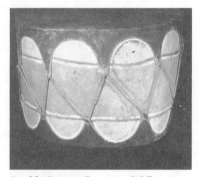

Pueblo Drum. Courtesy W.E. Channing & Co., Santa Fe.

In most tribes of North America, women were responsible for composing lullabies and spinning and grinding songs. But it was often the men (especially in Pueblo society) who kept time by beating with sticks or with their feet as the women worked, rocked, ground metates, and sang. On the Pacific coast, and in other areas as well, musical contests were held. Singers from one tribe (it could also be intratribal) would contend with those of another. The winner was the side who could remember the greatest number of songs, or who could accurately repeat a new song after hearing it for the first time. Among the Bafflin Land Eskimo, grudges were settled by opponents who sang derisive songs at one another. The one who earned the most laughter was the winner.

In ceremonial songs that made appeals to the deities or that celebrated their exploits, it was necessary for the singer(s) to achieve absolute accuracy. Otherwise, "the path would not be straight." An example of this may be noted in the following poem from *Sitting on the Blue-Eyed Bear: Navajo Myths and Legends:*

The Chanter's Failure

When the night chant fails nine times,
 I will step

into a piñon fire
  made by my own hands

San Ildefonso Singers. Photograph
by Joe Hedrick.

And, acknowledging my mistake,
 I will splash my bones
  with the flames of this fire.

Only after I have blackened myself with
 ash
and
 the fire has made me clean
  will the shame go away from
   my home.

A medicine man who makes a mistake while singing a sacred
song may cause the death of the patient. In some tribes, official
prompters kept strict watch during a ceremony to make sure the
singers did not make a mistake.

Pueblo Rattle. Courtesy W.E. Channing & Co., Santa Fe.

Northwest Coast Drum with Beater. Courtesy W.E. Channing & Co., Santa Fe.

The belief that breath is the symbol of life (as exemplified by "The Medicine Man of Jemez") is present in the act of singing. A voice lifted in song can carry the singer's life-breath into the eternal life-breath of life itself. Songs, chants, and prayers are used to address the Creator, the primary deities, the life-breath of life.

Native American singing is accompanied by skin drums, gourd rattles, bone whistles, and wooden flutes. If the drum may be considered the symbol of Mother Earth's heartbeat, then the whistle and flute may be symbolic of the wind (life-breath). The rattle is a symbol of cricket, locust, and snake, as well as the drone-sound given off by the elements of rain, hail, and wind-driven snow.

The Osage singer who sang of these things spoke of the tall grass moving in the wind, the bull snake making his own good song:

The great snake that makes a buzzing
 sound
Makes a sound like the blowing of the wind—
Close to the feet of the sick he moves
 sounding
His rattle close to the head of the sick
 sounding
His rattle
    toward the east winds
    toward the west winds
    toward the winds of cedars
Into the days of peace and beauty
 when men
Make of me their bodies
 in the days
Of peace and beauty that will come.

NAME

◆ ◆ ◆

Names were given, taken, or received during a propitious time in the life of an Indian. The name-giving time was generally at birth, puberty, and whenever an individual distinguished himself in the eyes of the tribe.

Here are a few examples of the variance in name giving within several different North American tribes:

A Mojave child who was born out of wedlock received an "ancient name" that was not commonly used in the tribe.

A Delaware child was often named for a dream that had come to his/her father.

A Maidu child might be named for an incident that happened at the time of birth. However, if no such incident took place, the child was referred to as "child, baby, boy." When the child was old enough to exhibit a name-giving characteristic, the name was then applied. If the child was a boy, the father and mother addressed him by his boyhood name all of his life. When the child was a girl, however, she was given a succession of names during the following times of her life: childhood, puberty, old age.

A Thlingchadinne man changed his name after the birth of each successive child. An unmarried man of the same tribe was known as the child of his favorite dog.

Kiowa names were bestowed by the grandparents. Young men, as they were growing up, usually took "dream names," which were

given them on quests of the spirit or through normal dreaming.

The name of honor was received after a person had attained some kind of special distinction in the tribe. This would occur through the performance of an act of great character, or it could be given by a secret society. The second name marked a moment of excellence in a person's life and was not an hereditary position. Hereditary names, such as that of an Iroquois chief, were passed down successively to whoever filled the position for as long as there were people to fill it.

Indian names could be loaned, pawned, given, or even thrown away. They might also be adopted out of revenge, without consent of the owner. The use of a name was somewhat guarded, in that it was considered discourteous or even insulting to address one directly by it. Because of the sacred nature of the name, a man might not offer his designation to another man but would ask a third party to speak it for him. In many tribes, custom prohibited a man from directly addressing his wife, his mother-in-law, and sometimes his father-in-law. This custom also worked in reverse.

Translating Indian names often creates errors not found in the original language. The Kiowa chief Bear Bearing Down was translated into English as Stumbling Bear. *Hajo,* a Creek war title, which means "recklessly brave," was rendered as "Crazy." Some names, when translated to a shortened form, wind up incorrect. For example, in Kiowa, *Takaibodal* means He Who Fights So Much He Does Not Have Time to Change His Saddle Blanket. This name was incorrectly shortened in English to Stinking Saddle Blanket. The Dakota chief Young Man Whose Very Horses Are Feared was given the literal English translation of Young Man Afraid of His Horses. (It has also been suggested, however, that Indian names contain irony, and that since the above name, for example, places particular emphasis on this, the latter translations here are correct. Another possibility is that names carry cultural associations that seem to defy definitive translation. I side with those who feel the English words do not do justice to the original.)

Opposite: Magpie-Cheyenne.
Photograph by Edward S. Curtis.
Courtesy Rainbow Man, Santa Fe.

Robert Boissiere, one of the only white men to have lived as an Indian at Taos Pueblo, told the story of how he received his Indian name from his Taoseño wife, Mary:

I was struck by the place, my head bent backward to have a complete view of the waterfall. When I looked at Mary she was smiling.

"So this is the place," I said.

"Yes," she answered.

I was overwhelmed.

She had brought the feather of a spotted eagle, a feather she had worn many times when in her buckskin clothes.

Standing together under the waterfall, she let the water fall on the eagle feather, blessing my head and the different parts of my body. I felt strong currents of energy going through my body as she did it.

"Your name will be *Ghiapateuh*," she said in a loud voice, "White Feather."

Her head turned toward the sky, her voice addressing the spirit world.

The Naming of Names

Chickasaw, Choctaw
Creek, Shawnee

Mandan, Kickapoo
Sioux, Zuni

How many names can we name?
The People called The People
Where have they gone to?
What have they got to do
Now that they're so few?

Lie down and die
Get up and try
Here's mud in your eye.

Chickasaw
Choctaw
Creek Shawnee

Micmac Mohawk
Pottawattomi

Where did the last Algonquin go?
Over there, somewhere
By that rabbit snare
Called the Bronx, some time ago.
Don't you know
We put him under glass
We mailed him fourth class

We put him on the stamp
We sent him down the ramp
But no one's to blame
There's no shame
A deal's
Not a steal:
Wait a minute, Peter Minuit
Didn't you buy
Manhattan
For sixty guilders
Worth of articles?

Ramapo
Chicago
Mankato

Geronimo
May we borrow your name
For our own gain?
You won't miss it
After we're through with it.
May we take your land
For a shake of the hand?
You won't want it
After we're through with it

Manhattan
Manhattan
Manhattan
Manhattan

Old "island of hills"
Plagued with ills
Sold to a nation of builders
For 60 guilders

What Algonquin ghost
Dances on your city
Of homeless
Home-makers,
Broken down
Contractors,
Name-swindling
Fast-talkers,
Land-gobbling
Money-lenders,
Doomsday idlers
In the canyons
Of the damned
Where once

Opposite: Man on the Cloud—Cheyenne. Photograph by Edward S. Curtis. Courtesy Rainbow Man, Santa Fe.

the Dutch played football
with the severed head of
an Indian chief?

Old ghost,
Can you forgive
this name-stealing nation
Of people
Who never had
The courage
To call themselves
The People?

OBSIDIAN

◆ ◆ ◆

Black or blackish in color, obsidian is a volcanic glass that many tribes adopted for a variety of uses. In addition to dark obsidian—the most common kind—there are also brown, green, red, and even mottled pieces that were used for implements and ornaments, sacred and decorative. Large bodies of it have been found in the western part of North America, especially in Yellowstone Park. Although extremely rare in the eastern United States, a remarkable deposit of obsidian implements was found in a burial mound near Hopewell Farm, near Chillicothe, Ohio.

In the Pacific states, beautifully shaped knife blades, measuring more than thirty inches in length and five inches in width, have been unearthed. Delicately shaped arrow points and ceremonial flakes, knives, and other blades were still in use around 1900. These were used as wearable art; for a medium of exchange or trade; and for sacred or ceremonial purposes. The artisan who crafted an implement out of obsidian used a process of "pecking and grinding." The finished work was truly a work of art.

In a section of *Desert Notes,* Barry Lopez describes a lost tribe of fictional desert dwellers whose ability to utilize bizarre materials is both mystical and intriguing. He describes knives "made of silver and inlaid with black obsidian glass along the cutting edge." Though the so-called Blue Mound People Lopez describes are the creatures of fiction, their use of such an extravagant tool is not far-fetched at all.

Archaeologists who discovered obsidian objects were frequently astounded by their utility, beauty, and craft. They did not, according to the journals, appear to be implements of a "primitive society," but, rather, an advanced technological one.

It is interesting to note that the recent use of obsidian dental drills would not detract from this point of view. As a boy in the 1950s, I once made the discovery of an obsidian arrowhead. It was in a stream in the then-undeveloped hills of Watchung, New Jersey. What a thing it was: thin-edged, glassy, smoke-dipped, and hard as steel.

I don't know whether it was the last such point to be found in those hills, but I do know that within a few years, the hills themselves were leveled to make way for suburban homes. By the time I became a teenager, the stream where I had found the rare obsidian arrowhead was a bit of spittle running through a cement conduit.

Rainbow Obsidian

In a chunk of pink-brown rhyolite
A streak of rainbow obsidian shone
Spectrum in stone.
Life is the incarnation of light
Photosynthetic to the bottom of the sea.

A cloudburst ripped ravines down the mountains to the plains,
Flooded arroyos and sagebrush flats,
Cleared except for a drizzle where
Two rainbows blazed in the ozone air
And under the lower arc was hung
A veil of violet mist that clung
On the sage and the hills and mountains and sky . . .
    —From *Rainbow Obsidian* by Phillips Kloss

PARROT

◆ ◆ ◆

At the Santo Domingo Corn Dance, one sees parrot feathers tied in bunches in the hair of the male dancers. In August, against the background of desert heat, shimmering sunlight, and the women dancing with sprigs of spruce, the parrot feathers are a striking contrast.

One asks, Where do they come from? What ancient symbol do they call forth?

The male dancers also wear fox skins at their waist and skunk fur around their moccasin boots, but these are animals native to the Southwest. Where do the parrots come in?

It is said that the ancestors of the Pueblo people came from Mexico, that they migrated in various clans or branches of the mother tribe into the dry Southwest. Yet, it is also said that hundreds of years ago, the grass of New Mexico was "belly deep to a horse," and it was a far more fertile place to live. With the wanderers, one might suppose, came the root culture of their former home, the jungle.

Parrot feathers: red, green, gold and blue. Primary colors of Native America. Aside from their obvious beauty, what might these sprigs of earth life from a tropical clime represent? Anyone who owns or has owned an Amazon parrot, for instance, knows that they live as much on seed as on rain. Carriers of seed in the tropics—as the moth to the night flower, the bee to the day blos-

Blue-Fronted Amazon Parrot.
Photograph by Bobbe Besold.

som—parrots are also the loud daily proclaimers of the coming of rain. They cannot live without a daily shower.

And it is this, I think, which gives the parrot feather a special symbolism in the Southwest, where rain (the Santo Domingo Corn Dance literally produces it) is the sacred element of life. Without it, nothing can live. The feathers are prayers representing hard tropic rain.

Once, while talking to a Tesuque Pueblo man, I was told that parrot feathers were not brought up through migrations from the south but came up continually, carried by runners to the pueblos. And not just feathers, he said, all kinds of things were brought: plants, seeds, designs, whatever was needed for trade. The old trade routes, he explained, were as active as any of today's highways.

PEYOTE

◆ ◆ ◆

Similar to the Ghost Dance religion, the Native American Church, which relies on Peyote as an integral part of its ritual, is a latter-day religion of Native America. The uncertainty of the old ways brought back mysticism in an old style, new faith format. As in the Ghost Dance, peyote and the Native American Church have been greatly misunderstood by the culture at large. With the ghost dance, the originator, Wovoka, a Paiute mystic who claimed to have died and been reborn, incorporated a message of peace into his teachings. Through the Ghost Dance, he believed, the remaining tribes of Turtle Island would reassemble their faith in their own intuitive ways. As an apostle of the Ghost Dance, Wovoka's teachings became popular with Indians around 1889. This was one year before the massacre at Wounded Knee, the beginning of the end, a time when the tribes would almost unilaterally lose faith in their right to live as Native Americans.

Peyote and its use by Indians is a very old practice. However, its incorporation into a specific ceremony for gaining religious insight in a communal way is not an old thing but one that is fairly recent. It has gained greater acceptance within the last fifty years through the Native American Church, whose purpose is similar to the Ghost Dance religion: to bring back the spirit of Indian America through mystic revelation.

The word *peyote* comes from the Nahuatl, *peyotl,* or "caterpil-

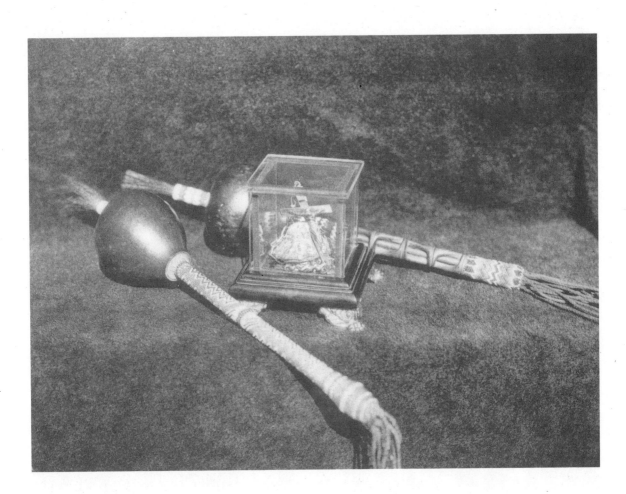

lar," referring to the downy center or button of the peyote cactus. Found in the lower Rio Grande area, and southward into Mexico, the peyote plant, as it is also known, has been used by Indians for ceremonial and medicinal purposes for hundreds of years. The Kiowa called it *seni*, the Comanche, *wokowi*, the Tarahumara, *hikori* or *hikuli*. In appearance, the peyote plant looks like a radish, with only the top appearing above ground. From the center springs a beautiful white blossom, which is later displaced by a tuft of white down.

The use of peyote buttons in the Native American Church is

Osage Peyote Rattles and Shrine. Photograph by Edward S. Curtis. Courtesy Rainbow Man, Santa Fe.

Kiowa Peyote Fan. I.A.I.A.
Museum Collection.

central to its philosophy. The ceremony involves ingestion of peyote, the singing of prayer songs, and also quiet contemplation. Traditionally, the meetings took place in a tepee with twenty-one poles, and the doorway facing east. The ceremony, which begins in the evening, continues until the sun rises in the east. A fire of seven cedar sticks touching at the points is kept burning in the center of the tepee by the Fire Chief. Other leaders of the ceremony are the Peyote Chief, Drum Chief, Cedar Man. The peyote button, referred to as Our Father Peyote, is placed upon a crescent-shaped mound. The participants, usually men, sit in a circle. Together they are brothers of the peyote-eater circle, traveling on the peyote road of life.

Just as the men start out by eating four peyote buttons, so they also sing four songs, and thus, into the night of visions, the ritual is continued, always moving, sunwise, from the left and going in a circle. At daylight, the morning star song is sung and then a ritual feast is begun.

There is nothing new in the ceremony; even the ingestion of peyote is an old practice. What gives it a unique place in Native American contemporary history is that, like the Buffalo Dance, the Sun Dance, and the Ghost Dance, the peyote ritual takes a firm hold of the Native American mind, a mind that has, despite the genocide that has tried to wipe it out, a firm hold in Mother Earth. Where the Christian Church failed to impress the ancientness of this mind, the older, adaptable religions of the last hundred years have planted seeds of their own.

As an antidote for alcoholism and a call to the inner needs of the Indian, the peyote road and even the marijuana Rasta road are good traveling. The disintegration of the old ways leaves the youth confused and embittered about where to go and what to do—and, fundamentally, how to be. Rastafarianism, promulgated by the poet-prophet of reggae, Bob Marley, has also had a profound effect on young people within the pueblos, as well as on other tribes. It is interesting that all of these "old-new" religions have at their core a sense of brotherhood and unity within the tribal universe. The assumption is that man is not alone; he is merely a member of one large tribe, all men being equal. This was Wovoka's message, not "red supremacy," and this was Bob Marley's message, not "black separatism," and this was the word of Handsome Lake, the Iroquois messiah who spread the gospel of an Indian Christ.

Here is a poem of the harmony road, the way that leads back into ourselves and out again into the world of man and woman:

Martiniano, the man who killed the deer

The prairie moon was rising
Wind blew cross the sage
Cars & pickups pulled up
Taos, Kiowa, Osage

Chanting through the night
In the eerie tepee glow
Sparks danced up the smokehole
To the stars with Mescalito

All night old Martiniano
Sat straight and tall
Till the morningbird arose
To meet the dawn that Fall.
                    —Sid Hausman

PIPE

♦ ♦ ♦

The Native American pipe was made of a variety of things: clay, stone, bone, steel, and iron. It assumed all shapes and sizes, but primarily it was a tube in which, usually but not always, tobacco, the scared herb, was smoked. Some pipes were straight; others were curved. Some had two or more bowls or stems, while others had detachable parts.

The purpose of the pipe was mainly to draw smoke into the mouth and release it. Ceremonially, this was done by first blowing the smoke to the cardinal directions. Indian pipes have long been associated with peacemaking. However, there were war pipes, as well. Pipes of great size have been discovered by archaeologists. Some of these, weighing several pounds apiece, were used to make treaties and seal various kinds of trade agreements or alliances. In every Indian village or community, there was a skilled artisan whose knowledge of pipe making was respected. The material most commonly sought for pipe making was soapstone, but many other materials were also used.

The word *calumet,* which was associated with the name of a dance, later became identified with the designation for the pipe. In 1724, a French explorer referred to the calumet as the true altar of sacrifice for addressing the deity of the sun. One of the most

Haida Pipe Bowl. Courtesy W.E. Channing & Co., Santa Fe.

famous pipes was the hatchet or tomahawk pipe. It was used as a light tool and also for a ceremonial implement. The head was made of metal, while the stem might be made of wood or metal, or both. The tomahawk was used for ceremonies of war and peace, chopping and smoking.

PUEBLO

•   •   •

The term *pueblo* was first applied by the Spaniards and later adopted by English-speaking people to designate Indians who lived in permanent stone and adobe houses. Today, there are permanently occupied pueblo villages in Arizona and New Mexico. These include Tanoan, Keresan, Zunian, and Hopi-Shoshonean linguistic families.

Of the pueblo tribes, the Zuni were the first to become known to the Spanish conquerors of New Mexico. In 1539, Fray Marcos of Niza, a Franciscan, journeyed northward from the city of Mexico. With him was a Barbary black man named Estevan (Estevanico). This man had been a companion of the legendary conquistador-turned-healer, Cabeza de Vaca. According to plan, Estevan traveled ahead of the friar to prepare the way for him. However, when he reached the Zuni villages of western New Mexico, Estevan took advantage of the hospitality of his hosts and was imprisoned by them. Later they took him outside the pueblo and killed him. The rest of pueblo history—not only Zuni but all of the pueblos—is one long dreary account of conquest and reprisal. In the end, to appease the conquerors, the Indians adopted Spanish customs and procedures, but they kept the integrity of their religion, their clan system, their way of life. The concession to the Spanish was in name only. For this reason, the pueblos are functioning today the way they did many hundreds of years ago. Frank Waters has

described the process of Spanish colonization and even Anglo interference as being, metaphorically, a wave breaking over a rock. Here, from Indian eyes, is how Loren Straight Eagle Plume sees it:

Unscathed Eyes

In Fall,
Jemez people gather at the pueblo
we come to feast and dance
    and talk to old friends

Outside in the forest
All seems relative
related to me, I'm not a
centerpiece
    but I've become an instrument
    an aspect of earth's personality

Old Fords
rumble, squeak, and clank on dusty roads
I don't quite understand the new ways
the young ones head for the TVs
no rationality
I watch the old ones
in colorful blankets move toward the kiva
in the cold evening
I'm losing the "Old Ways"

Instability
  is something new
  to the Native American world

We dream
  of what could and will be

Taos Pueblo. Photograph by Joe
Hedrick.

We become
  our true selves
it will be as I see
  our intuitions grow

here, we will survive
  but never flourish
  here, we will die
    but never remain

Somewhere in time
    this continent is undisturbed

There, in those wooded highlands
  I'm watching Jemez Pueblo with

    unscathed eyes

When the Spanish first saw the pueblos, they imagined them to be the fulfillment of the myth of the Seven Cities of Cibola. Perhaps the precise angle of sunlight shafting down over the sky city of Acoma created such a legend: The vast storehouses of golden wealth turned out, in any case, to be nothing more than storage vaults of corn. Today, the rectangular, enclosed, open-courted communities still resemble the ancient sun cities of Spanish myth.

Of course, not everything the Spanish introduced to pueblo life was bad. With the early colonists came sheep and with sheep came wool. The introduction of wool to the southwestern Indians was a major occurrence. Weaving became, in time, a major industry for the Pueblo people. Navajo weavers, considered to be among the finest in the world, learned their craft, it is believed, from Pueblo women who were captured and adopted into their tribe.

Pueblo life is organized around the communal grouping of two social units: Summer People and Winter People. Each group is watched over by a respective chief. During the winter months, the Summer People are subordinate to the Winter People, and vice versa. To each fall the seasonal responsibilities of the village and its welfare. The pattern of pueblo life is thus synonymous with the course of nature. In most pueblos, each group has its own kiva: one for Winter People and one for Summer People. Often there is yet one more kiva for ceremonies where both groups are united. In some pueblos, Taos, for example, there are multiple kivas.

Pueblo civil government is based on a system designed originally by the Spanish. Usually there is a governor, elected or appointed, every one or two years. He is assisted by one or two lieutenant governors and a sheriff. In addition there is an officer—a carryover from the Spanish style of government—a *fiscale*, who is responsible for matters of "church and state." There is also a war captain, the only civil officer who is also a religious figure. And, finally, there is a council made up of former governors.

What is the pueblo today if not the assemblage of things that it once was: "We dream/of what could and will be." The pueblo stays on, a living monument to the past, an uncreated dream of the future, in the minds of the men and women who live there. But the changes of life, the modernity factor, so to speak, alter the way the young interact with the old; the TV talks louder than wise old men. The poet says, "here we will survive/but never flourish/here we will die/but never remain," his eyes roving the highland hills looking for the mystic pueblo, the one where nothing changes because there is no change; the one where time does not exist.

Taos Pueblo

"We are made," he said, "of mud, straw, clay
and fire." He was going to say more, but he had work to do.
We watched the sun set behind him,
   the smoke speaking
from the many-chimneyed houses made of mud and straw.
The pueblo cast the same lean lines it had always cast.
Ladders going up walls in crazy angles.
   The old man carried his bucket down to the
stream. A small boy lay on the mud brown bank beside a wolf
with silver blue eyes. All day long
   the old man hauled water from the stream and the
boy slept next to the watching wolf.
   Sundown: a car with the crest of the Navajo nation
pulled up; two Navajo men sat inside
   smoking
cigarettes and watching, as we did,
the pueblo dusk, the mud order of simple squares
piled five stories into the sky. These were men with earth

Navajo Series. Number UN 24.09. Museum of Indian Arts and Culture/Laboratory of Anthropology, Santa Fe.

houses
built into the earth, men whose great grandfathers had plundered this pueblo for silver, blankets, meat and women.

In the car, the two men smoked and laughed at some
ancient joke.

The old man on the slippery bank
dipped his hundredth bucket of pueblo water into the stream of
his birth.

We saw in the Sangre de Cristo blood-light the
black chalk flakes of flame gone cold on the mountain's
 edge. The old man walked into the shadow of
Taos Mountain, and the blue fell like a blanket around
 his shoulders. As he disappeared we saw his
blanketed signature—nothing, and yet
 it was there
as he was there, walking into shadow.

QUILL

◆ ◆ ◆

Embroidery using porcupine quills or bird feathers was principal-
ly a craft of the Cheyenne, Arapaho, and Sioux. The hunting of
porcupines and the capture of birds was men's work. In some
tribes, men also prepared the dyes. Sorting and coloring the quills
and applying them to deerskin or birchbark was exclusively the
work of women.

The quills were steeped in concoctions of dye made from roots,
plants, buds, and bark. The standard uniform colors of the dyed
quill were red, yellow, green, blue, and black. Feather quills, all
except the fine pliant tips, were split; porcupine quills were
flattened.

Quillwork was used to decorate tobacco and tinder bags, work
bags, knife sheaths, cradles, amulets, shirts, leggings, belts, arm
and leg bands, moccasins, robes, and cases and boxes made of
birchbark. Porcupine quills were used for embroidery by tribes
from Maine to Virginia, west to the Rocky Mountains, and all the
way to the northwest Coast. Quills, as an item of barter, were not
confined to the regions where the animals themselves lived.

Decorative figures and designs in quill often expressed prayers
for safety, long life, and prosperity. Designs were borrowed from
tribe to tribe by women. There were designs, however, created by
men and those created by women; naturally there were also
designs common to both.

The art of quillwork seems to have flourished with greatest intensity in tribes where the porcupine was native. Since it was also an activity that demanded leisure, it was necessary that the women of the tribe had time to work in quill. This time could be provided only where there was a dependable food supply provided by the men.

In the 1950s, quillwork done by Indians was almost a dying art, with few practitioners on the reservations. Today, there has been a resurgence of interest in the art, due, in part, to the national shift in consciousness to the teaching of Native Americans. It is as if the quality of life in the United States had become so sterile that it had nowhere to turn but to the preceding century, which itself was a fall from grace from the century before. The preservation of lost arts and crafts is an important concern, and many Indian practices, once dropped in the rush to become "modern," are now experiencing renewal within the tribes.

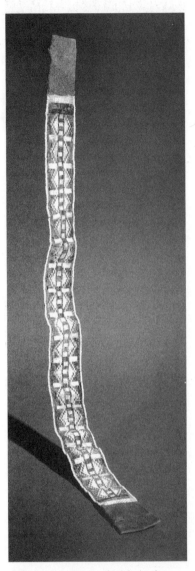

Athabascan Strap of Hide and Quillwork. Courtesy W.E. Channing & Co., Santa Fe.

RELIGION

• • •

The Moon Chant. Guy Nez (Navajo). I.A.I.A. Museum Collection.

As a symbol of things Native American, religion is both the most common—the mother symbol, if you will—and the most ambiguous. In Navajo, for example, there is no separate word for *religion;* it exists, as it does in most other tribes, in the heart of life as it is being lived. Of course, the Europeans who first came in contact with the people of Turtle Island treated the concept of religion as if it were a separate day of the week. It was hard for them to understand the animism of the Indian, the belief that *life* is the animate force of life. As one early anthropologist wrote: "The fundamental concept bearing on the religious life of the individual (Indian) is the belief in the existence of magic power. . . ."

The idea that magic is at the heart of Native American religion is absurd, and yet it persists as much today as it did at the turn of this century. That objects, animals, and men might interchange their identities was not a leap of the imagination for an Indian. For the outsider, however, such a belief coincided with a "primitive faith in magic," something that Europeans had not quite successfully discarded a century or two before. The concept of a higher power was acceptable to the outsider, but the Indian belief in multitudes of name-changing deities was not. So there remains to this day a block in understanding, made worse by fiction, television, and films that distort Native American wisdom, religion, and ceremonial practice.

To the Algonquian tribes the great force of life was called *Manito.* The Siouan tribes called the force *Wakanda.* The Iroquois word was *Orenda;* the Salish, *Sulia,* the Kwakiutl, *Nawalak.* The notion of the Great Spirit was something that the culture at large could understand, but only as it pertained to the narrow view of a particular Christian religion. The mystical god of the Old Testament, Yahweh, who speaks from clouds, flashes of light, flames, and whirlwinds, would have made a great deal of sense to most Native Americans—and, for that matter, did—but too often the parables of Jesus and His all-knowing Father were laid before them as the track on which the train must run. There was no room on this track for the expression of a faith in the trackless.

Apache Spirit Dancers. Photograph by Joe Hedrick.

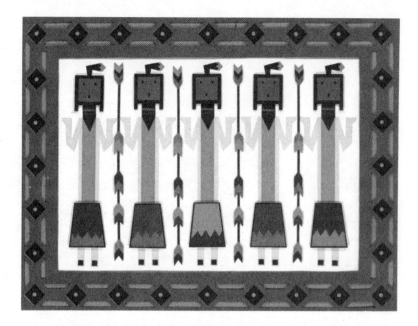

Yei Dancers. Paper collage. Roger H. Rodgers. Courtesy Sunstone Press.

Life, as the Indians knew it, was a great mystery. It could not be reduced to theology or logic.

As stated earlier, the Native American way encompasses many deities, all of them interrelated. Animals, men and women, insects, and other creatures are participants in a pageant that is cocreative. The lives of things are seen as passive, but as active members of a growing consciousness. The First World of the Navajo, for instance, was a world of darkness inhabited by nine people, six kinds of ants, and three kinds of beetles. Everyone spoke the same language. There were no stones, no vegetation, no light. It was a primary and simple world, but contained within it were the beginnings of actions and the desire for upward movement. There was no primary creator or God, making the world and life. Rather, creation came about from the stirrings of movement in the bottommost world, the first active step toward change, and continued until emergence in the Fifth World.

The Native American world view holds that all things are cast into the matrix of a living present. The belief does not deny a past or future, because these are fused into the present like the striations of schist in a bedrock. To the Navajo, the Rock with Wings, now called Shiprock, was once in ancient times a deity—part man, part bird—that turned into stone. Its spirit, a living thing, is active. Fused into the sacred rock are past, present, and future. The Rock with Wings "lives." This is its animistic nature, and, further, the animism of the Indian world. What does not live if the breath of life, the word, has been given to it? So said, in fact, the writer(s) of Genesis.

Power is a word often aligned (maligned, we should say) with magic. In most tribes, power was the consequence of synchronicity. An individual who lived in the "right" way was rewarded by the deities with whom he was in harmony. An individual who had fallen from the sense of his own well-being might well be deserted by these same deities. Thus, the man with and the man without power. Among the Arapaho and Blackfeet (Siksika), the privilege of power was actually purchased. For the American Eskimo, power could be transmitted through contact with a "person of power." In most tribes, power could be invoked through powerful dreams; through prayer, offering, and sacrifice. Power could also be gotten through visions brought on by privation and ritual, through the quest and the dance. Power might also be acquired through inheritance, passed on by an elder, given to one deserving of it. It could be attained in old age through wisdom. In truth, the terms magic and power are not good ones. Perhaps they should be replaced by an understanding of the concept of divine harmony. The Navajo say that when a man walks upon "the middle road," he avoids the weakening of his strength as a man:

If he does not put strain in his life
If he follows his father's path in wisdom
Pollen will shine in his smile.

Once, when I was exuberant about a "mystic message" I had received in a dream, I told a Navajo friend about it. He said that I should not talk about such things. I asked him why that was so. He said that when we speak of revelations, we are showing "our power" and that when we do this, the deities no longer feel that we need their help. By being quiet about such things, the deities remain with us, ready to help.

SACRIFICE

• • •

In Latin, *sacrifice* means "to make sacred." The present-day association with this word, however, is self-abnegation, or, to put it in the vernacular, to give up something for something. Paying homage to the deities was, and is, common to all Native American people. Pueblo Indians of today still make "fireplace offerings" when they are having a meal. The food, which is itself a blessing, a sacrifice, is given to "the grandfather of the fire" as homage and prayer. This custom was also practiced by the Natchez Indians, who always fed the deities before they themselves accepted food for a feast.

Offerings of various kinds, at various times, were given to the deities of sky, earth, sun, moon, wind, thunder, mountain, rock, animal, tree, rain, and river. Then, as now, however, it was not the thing itself to which the sacrifice was made but its spirit. Therefore, Navajo who give the gift of pollen to the sun are not making an offering to a planetary body but, rather, to the Sun Father, who, it is said, carries the planetary sun with him. Gifts of many kinds are used today as offerings: feathers, pollen, cornmeal, tobacco, shells, beads, and herbs:

Winter Prayer

Father of green dreams
  story me high
  on hawk's wings:
Summer me soon
  in high mountain meadow:
    goat-white clouds
    turquoise sky.
Leave me there, Father
  to juniper
  ever.

Long ago, Indians made sacrifices of animals and, sometimes, human beings. The Huron people, for instance, burned the viscera and a portion of the flesh of one who was drowned or who had died of a cold. The offering was given to the sky. The Skidi Pawnee sacrificed a female captive to the morning star and the Kansa Indians placed the hearts of slain foes into the fire as a sacrifice to the wind. The Sun Dance, common to the Plains tribes (and still practiced today, though without the sacrifices of former times) involved the hooking of thongs into the flesh (usually the breast of a man), and then drawing upon it. Self-mutilation also occurred in the Sun Ceremony—offerings of finger joints and flesh.

Tobacco is presently used, as it was historically, loose, powdered, and drawn as smoke through a pipe. Given to the four directions, zenith, and nadir successively, the act of smoking—by and of itself—can be interpreted as an act of prayer, a spiritual ceremony.

The deities of the river were shown obeisance by eastern tribes who made special offerings by every rock, rapid, and eddy that possessed the river deity's power. Alaskan Eskimos gave the skin of a slain animal to the moon, asking that she send more to them. Today, Navajo and Pueblo people use *pahos*, or "prayer feathers,"

to make offerings and give thanks. In a Mohawk prayer that I
heard recently, every deity of sky and earth was given thanks for
permitting the people to live. Those of us fortunate enough to
hear the prayer were thankful for the wood that made the chairs
given by the trees, which were, in turn, thankful for the sky and
the rain; all vibrant, life-supporting elements were praised and
given thanks for permitting us to share their blessing with them.

The time and nature of sacrifice is important to Native
Americans. Some sacrifices are spontaneous, but most are
ordained by season. Not long ago, a Santo Domingo Pueblo

Black Hawk. Monotype. Ross Lew
Allen.

In the Medicine Lodge—Arikara.
Photograph by Edward S. Curtis.
Courtesy Rainbow Man, Santa Fe.

woman told me that she had visited an American Indian art gallery where she saw many personal belongings of ancestors— cradle boards, moccasins, and clothes. Shocked that these things were on display and feeling that they were not in their rightful place, she made an offering of cornmeal and rinsed her mouth with water to cleanse herself of the sight. This prayer of the moment helped her get through a painful experience.

However, while such offerings are perhaps a daily practice among Indians, the larger, group-oriented sacrifices are coordinated with time and season. The White Dog Feast of the Iroquois was celebrated five days after the first appearance of the new moon following the winter solstice. The corn-planting ceremony of the Quawpaw was dependent upon the succession of the season, as was the Ntlakyapamuk sacrifice of the first berries of the season. Storytelling, tribal fashion, also done seasonally, is a kind of sacrifice to the deities who first provided the stories, or the reason to tell them. Winter stories are not to be told in summer; otherwise, the pattern of life is out of harmony. Native American stories are not, therefore, idle entertainment; they are educational lessons for the young, spiritual reminders for all ages, giving guidance and counsel lest one forget one's place. Nor is it ever forgotten that the inspiration of the story, and that of the storyteller, is given by the deities whose story, in truth, it is.

The Sweat Lodge

Night of cedar smoke and snowflake, sitting in the sweat-
  lodge, barefoot, in the dark
    listening
Naked to the voice of the elder
    saying
Thank you, over and over, for being alive, thank you, for
  walking
  waking
  wondering
  wanting
  working
Thank you. The hours and prayers go by in the darkness and
  time is marked by the clacking of deer-antlers, sparks
  dancing around the hot lava rocks, the sweat
    trickling
Drop at a time, down the spine-bone, knobby as a snake

in the dark. And still the smoke-master elder moves
through cedar smoke and snowflake blessing each thing:
the ice-water poured over the naked head and back,
  splashing
The soul with gratefulness, genuine pleasure at the hurt
  startled bone-
    shaking
  jump of the flesh each time the water
Poured over the head under the stars
  winking
And the lazy snow flakes
  tilting
Down and the cedar sparks
  cracking
upward on this night of sweating and thanking and praying and
  being
This night of cedar smoke and snow flake,
  in the first hiss of life, fire on rock, fire in sky
  fire in the first soul of man and woman,

Snow flake and cedar smoke, prayer and answer, salt of body,
  sugar of hope, lesson in the
  listening
  loving
Nightfall, snowfall.

SHELL

♦ ♦ ♦

Shell was, and still is, widely used in Native American craft and art. It was used in former times for making utensils as well as ornaments. Among the tribes north of Mexico, clam and mussel shells were used as cups and spoons. These were also hafted for scraping and digging implements, and they were carved into fishhooks and knives. The large conchs were used as drinking vessels, and when the interior shell was removed, they were used by Florida tribes as clubs and pickaxes. Abalone on the Pacific coast was cut, trimmed, ground, polished and perforated for beads, pins, pendants, and breastplates. Along the Atlantic coast, clam shells were made into cylindrical beads strung out as necklaces and also woven into belts. In the time of the first colonists, the Indians were using shell belts almost exclusively as a medium of exchange known as wampum.

Leopard Cowrie. Photograph by Bobbe Besold.

Belts of wampum may have their contemporary corollary in today's money belt. But in the sixteenth century, and for some time afterward, shell belts were traded and used outright as money by coastal tribes who bartered with their inland brothers. The most widely used "money shell" was the cowry. (The ringed cowry was used on remote Indian and Pacific islands well into the 1950s. Along the west coast of Africa, strings of "money cowry" were standard currency until past the middle of the nineteenth century.)

Wampum was made of cylindrical fragments of quahog, whelk, and periwinkle shells rubbed smooth on stones and strung like beads on fine strands of skin. The white beads were generally rated at half the value of the purple beads, which were cut from the quahog, or hard clam. Wampum remained an accepted medium of trade until far into the eighteenth century. A seventeenth-century English author, describing the contents of the holds of two trade ships in London Harbour, said that the ships were fully laden with curious little shells.

Opposite: Navajo Woman and Child. Smithsonian Collection.

Big Shell Man

The iridescent abalone shell, the big shell brought from the
    Coast by early Indian traders,
Symbol of great water, sea water, sky water, a fragment of the
    rainbow held in hand,
Gave name to the main kiva on the north, and its chief was
    called Big Shell Man.
He was well-qualified to be chief, a natural leader, powerful
    physique, powerful mind.
He wore his blanket toga-like, wore his hair in neat-tied chonga,
    made his own moccasins of deerhide and elkhide,
Spoke quietly in the soft Tigua tongue, his eloquence so poetic
    the interpreter had to grope for the right words to render it
    into English.
His purpose was to hold his people together, to keep them to
    the Indian way of life,
And our friendship, he said, was like the wind between the willows and the pines, his people breathing the same spirit
    our people did. Not perverse, he accepted the White Man's
    tractor and plough as a logical improvement on the
    digging stick,
Cut his alfalfa with a mowing machine, fed his cattle in winter
    with hauled hay.

Two beautiful daughters he had, and two sons as wide-
shouldered and wide-minded as he was, well-trained in
tribal lore.

The daughters stayed at the Pueblo, the sons he sent to college
to read the great books in which the White Man stored
his thinking.

The older one mastered Herbert Spencer's synthetic philosophy,
translated the gist to his father, the evolutionary principles,
the curious belief in higher and higher development.

Yes, a child develops into a man, but the White Man develops
into a crazy child running around in big crazy cities.

Big Shell Man considered big cities the wrong way to live,
questioned himself what was the right way, the real way.

Neither the White Man's religion nor the Indian religion
satisfies the sense of reality.

El Senor Jesu Cristo, the Spanish son of God, could walk on
water and bring the dead back to life; no real man could.

Pai-an-quet-ta-tol-la, the Indian Red Person who shone like the
sun, could fly straight up in the sky like a copper-colored
hummingbird; no real man could.

Big Shell Man walked on earth, his flight of fancy returned to
earth like a luminous dream.

Hold on to your land, my sons, my daughters, hold on to your
land, my people,

Go up in the mountains, make an Indian shrine, think your
own thoughts, belong to yourself,

Live with the earth, live with the sky, hold the rainbow in your
hand.

  —From *The Great Kiva* by Phillips Kloss

SHIELD

♦ ♦ ♦

The shield of the mounted warrior of the Plains is an image commonly associated with Native American symbology. Plains Indian shields, roughly two feet in diameter, were made of thick buffalo hide, with one or two covers of soft-dressed buffalo, elk, or deerskin. The design on the outside cover was different from the inside cover. In battle, the warrior loosened and threw back the outside shield cover to reveal the secret symbol within. The shield was then carried on the left arm by means of a belt that passed over the shoulder. Carried in this fashion, the shield permitted the free use of the left hand to hold a bow, and it also allowed the shield to be slung around to the back, in retreat. It was sufficient to stop an arrow or the stroke of a lance, but it offered little protection against a bullet.

The warrior shield of the Plains Indian was, like a samurai's sword, his most sacred possession. From its first encounter with an enemy to the time when it was laid under its owner's head in death, the shield was a thing of power, having originated from a medicine dream. In the dream, often received by an old warrior, the young man was seen being instructed in the making and use of his shield. The shield had to be made according to the dream: painted and decorated in keeping with the wishes of the Shield Spirit. The spirit might be a bird, an animal, or a deity of the tribe.

The owner rarely made his own shield; instead, he received it

Shields. Fred Yazzie (Navajo). I.A.I.A. Museum Collection.

from the dreamer, who made it in trade for horses, blankets, or other property. To make the shield, the protective hide was taken from the neck of a buffalo bull. Extra thickness and toughness were created by wetting and shrinking the hide over a fire built over a hole in the ground. When it was not in use, the warrior's shield was often hung on a tripod of wooden poles that faced the sun.

SIGN

• • •

As a child, I learned sign language and woodland sign from my mother, who had learned them from her mentor, Ernest Thompson Seton. Following the little piles of stones in the forest correctly meant that at the end of the trail there would be a bag of sweets hanging from a branch. The pleasure of eating the candy, tied in a kerchief, was not as great as the joy of coming upon it and knowing that the sign reading had been done well. It was good, however, sitting in the woods under hickory and oak, watching the sun in the leaves and sucking on Hershey's chocolate.

Native Americans used hand sign as well as trail sign to communicate with members of other tribes with whom they did not share a common language. Gestures, mainly with the hands but also with the body, delivered a main system of communication for Indians between the Missouri River and the Rocky Mountains, and from the Fraser River in British Columbia south to the Rio Grande in New Mexico.

Just as human speech developed from a pictorial or ideographic origin, so sign language began as pantomimic movement reflecting the natural world. It may be described, in fact, as a form of pictograph in motion. Crow, Cheyenne, and Kiowa people were said to have been the most expert in the use of sign. The fluent grace of conversational sign language between Cheyenne and

Kiowa was, according to one observer, "the very poetry of motion."

The question "How old are you?" would become the following in sign language movements:

1. Point finger at subject= YOU
2. Cold sign= WINTER YEAR
3. Counting sign= NUMBER
4. Question sign= HOW MANY

An expert in sign language could phrase the above in the time it would take to say it.

Sign

She left a lifetime of sign; on hickory bark
  on the lake shore—little curls of birch,
  a chunk of pink quartz looking like ice cream
  frozen on the trail going up to the
  four-masted white pine by the cabin.
At the end of her life, she left without sign.
  There was nothing to follow, not even a
  bent twig we could follow.
  I remember the horseback trackers
  who lost her tracks in a snowstorm.

Somewhere in the wet flakes and bowed-down
  junipers, she'd given them the slip.
  Turned up at the Hilton, sipping port
  some eight hours later, with her dog
  hooked to her wrist with six-pack plastic.

After she died, I remember how she always
doubled-back. That secret, her finest
even the way she went out: curled-up
in fetal crouch like the little girl
who rubbed graves to wake the people up.

TOBACCO

♦ ♦ ♦

One of the sacred herbs of Turtle Island was tobacco. Used to make offerings to the deities, to treat disease, and to seal agreements, tobacco was also smoked for enjoyment. The word came originally from the Guarani, *taboca*, and it was allegedly first seen by Christopher Columbus on October 14, 1492. According to journal entries, an Indian man was observed traveling from Santa Maria to Fernandina—the second and third Bahama islands—with a canoe full of dry tobacco leaves. Messengers sent by Columbus stated that on the island of Cuba men took smoke "inside with the breath, by which they became benumbed and almost drunk, and so it is said they do not feel fatigue."

Between 1541 and 1546, the explorer Benzoni encountered Ethiopian slaves who had been brought to the West Indies by the Spanish. According to his report, the slaves took a leaf of maize and a leaf of another plant that "grows in these new countries" and rolled them tightly together. Benzoni said that after the recipients took the smoke, they would "fall down as if they were dead, and remain the greater part of the day or night stupefied." Others who smoked the same herb, he continued, "are content with imbibing only enough of this smoke to make them giddy, and no more."

In 1574, Nicolas Monardes called the plant he found on the islands tobacco. The word stuck. And the mysterious plant was

A Smoke—Arapaho. Photograph by Edward S. Curtis. Courtesy Rainbow Man, Santa Fe.

credited with wonderful properties, curing not only disease but also open wounds. Extolled as an intoxicant, a preventative of hunger and thirst, it was even said to ward off disease.

What of the uses of tobacco on Turtle Island at this time? Archaeologists have found votive offerings of sacred cigarettes in cave shrines that date back hundreds of years. It is doubtful that the plant was not being used in the places where it grew naturally, and it is probable that tobacco came into the Southwest through trade channels originating in the jungles of the Yucatán. Parrot feathers came into the desert that way, and even, so the Pueblo Indians say, fresh shrimp, wrapped in moss and carried by runners from the Texas coast.

The ceremonial mixing of tobacco and *ganga* (marijuana) is a custom shared by Afro-Jamaican people and the Native Americans of Turtle Island. I have spent time with members of the Havasupai, who live in the Grand Canyon of Arizona, and the younger tribesmen are, many of them, Rastafarian. Asked how long their "Rasta roots" had been connected to the island of Jamaica, one man commented, "Since creation." Taking him literally, as well as figuratively, I asked how this was possible, for the side canyon where he and his people lived was extremely isolated.

He answered that the Colorado River was not far from where we stood. "From there," he said, smiling, "you can go to Mexico." Since I had once seen the lights of Havana on a clear day in Cozumel, I knew that it was not impossible to get to Jamaica (roughly ninety miles from Cuba's shore) from Mexico, even by canoe, if one had to travel that way. This was an anthropological leap of the imagination, however: Did my friend want me to believe, literally, that his people and natives of the island of Jamaica had been swapping culture since the days of the Arawak? I asked, and he answered, "Yes." When I remarked that this would be hard for some of my colleagues to accept, he replied that if I were referring to white anthropologists, there was no telling what they might or might not accept. "We," he said, "have accepted these things because to us, they are not strange."

Sometime after the visit to Havasu, I was traveling on the island of Jamaica, where I witnessed a Rastafarian ceremony. Before the chanting, there was a ritual of rolling a corn-husk cigarette and filling it with sensemilla. This mixing of the two sacred plants of the Americas interested me. I was told by an herbsman there that he had learned the custom from his grandfather, who had learned it from his—all the way back to the Arawak, who showed it to the first slave who had traveled the Middle Passage. "These things," he said, "are our heritage. We believe them."

It is interesting to note that the "American heritage" of tobacco has also taken a kind of legendary turn. The toll of lung cancer from the obsessive smoking of cigarettes is one of the worst diseases in the United States. Of course, this very thing was predicted long ago by the shaman of the Plains. "Leave the white man be," they said, "for he will surely die of his own natural causes." This, I am sure, meant "by his own excesses." The overindulgence of tobacco in this country is as old as its inception. If one looks back to the colonies, the record is bleak even at the start. The cultivation of tobacco to the exclusion of other vegetal products brought the colonies of Virginia and Maryland to the verge of starvation more than once.

TOMAHAWK

• • •

The weapon tomahawk came from the Algonquian tribes of the eastern part of Turtle Island. Early writers in Virginia cite the word variously: *Tommahick, tomahack, tamahake, tamahaac.* However it is spelled, the name seems to fit. Virginia dialect probably transfigured the original Indian word, as it definitely did in the case of *tommyhawk.* The Algonquian use of the word is seen in the Cree word for hammer: *ootommoheggun.*

Plains Pipe Tomahawk. Courtesy W.E. Channing & Co., Santa Fe.

The tomahawk, decorated with feathers and engravings, was an implement of ceremony as well as warfare. Colonial writers spoke of the tomahawk as an "inscription device," whereon the owner recorded the pictographs of marches, battles, and other illuminating events. It was spoken of as ". . . a stout stick about three feet in length, terminating in a large knob, wherein a projecting bone or flint was often inserted." One Early American writer gallantly insisted that the tomahawk's origin was Gallic, because he claimed to have found one in his Virginia cornfield that was identical to one he had found in the potato fields of his farm in Ireland.

It is a known fact that the hatchet/pipe, the tomahawk with the head of steel, had a very definite and traceable European influence. It became known as "the tomahawk of trade," a symbol as well known as the "Indian blanket."

TOTEM

♦ ♦ ♦

Zia Olla. Courtesy W.E. Channing & Co., Santa Fe.

The word *totem* was irregularly derived from the term *ototeman* of the Chippewa, signifying, generically, "his brother/sister kin." From the root *ote* was added the concept of the animal that was the ordinary subsistence of the clan. Thus the animal itself became the symbol of each family and the perpetual symbol of each clan.

In Cree, *ototema* means "his relations" and indicates the Algonquian *otem* or the idea of making one's "mark."

"Enter, then, my mark" might be translated as "Enter, then, my clansman."

The "family mark" might be said to mean "the clan patron spirit."

The term *totem* in English usage has been indiscriminately applied to any number of "imaginary beings" who are the guardian spirits of a person or group of persons. The difficulty here is to try to separate the personal guardian, the family or clan guardian, and the societal guardian. The distinguishing features of these three totems are as follows:

A personal guardian is one obtained through rite of passage of dream, vision, personal experience.

A family or clan guardian is one passed on through lineage (although it may have originated as above).

A societal guardian is one that has been experienced not by blood kin but by others in the tribe who have a shared bond with that same guardian.

There is, in the Indian world, no conflict here, quite the contrary. As expressed by Jay de Groat:

my people

we are many clearly of different clans
we are one by our same belief
we have beauty behind us
we have beauty before us

we are the child of whiteshell woman
   to the east
we are the child of turquoise woman
   to the south
we are the child of abalone woman
   to the west
we are the child of jet woman
   to the north

we are white corn; father and son
we are yellow corn; mother and daughter
we harvest corn, we feast
we offer pollen, when we feast . . .

An explorer who lived among the Chippewa in 1855 said that every member of the tribe seemed to "deify a natural object in which he had confidence." This object—tree, rock, mountain—was literally a translation in Chippewa of "my hope." Another possible translation of this might be "my faith" or "my kinship."

In the Omaha tribe, a young man's rite of passage was to go off

Petroglyphs. Smithsonian Collection.

by himself to a secluded spot in the wilderness. There, chanting, praying, crying for a vision until trance or sleep overtook him, he waited for a certain thing to present itself. When the vision came, he returned home, where he would remain quiet for four days. It was important for him not to mention his vision, lest he lose its benefaction. However, later on, after the passing of days, he might speak of it, perhaps to an elder who had experienced a similar thing. Then it became the young man's duty—if his vision was of a bird, animal, or known presence in the natural world—to hunt the creature and slay it. After this was done, he would keep a small part of it in his medicine bundle. If, on the other hand, the youth did not encounter a "being of nature" in his vision but, rather, something more of the spirit world, then his search would be to find a symbol, in the natural world, that might represent it. The token could be a feather, tuft of grass, pebble, or strand of animal hair.

In either case, the young man, after completing his rite of passage, did not worship his totem or tutelary spirit. He kept it close to his heart; he talked to it; he borrowed its power or wisdom. However, he did not bow to it, beg its blessing, or ask it to accomplish things for him. Nor was he, during his time of privation, permitted to ask "the being" to present itself or to show him where he might find it, or something of its nature (feather, grass, pebble, etc.). These things should occur naturally, in their own time.

Unlike the Omaha, the Iroquois did not contemplate killing the object of their vision in order to obtain a part of it as token, or symbol. In Iroquois belief, the vision tutelary was so inextricably bound to the man or woman who had envisioned it that their lives were literally dependent upon one another. If the totem, for instance, happened to be a guardian animal, then the man guarded the animal as much as the animal guarded the man. The Iroquoian and Algonquian belief stemmed from the idea that every animal being had an elder brother, a primal being, whose blessing must be sought on the hunt. It was thus the favor of the elder brother of the animal who gave favor to the hunter.

Here, in the words of Loren Straight Eagle Plume, is a rite of passage, a transformation that happened to him. The change he experienced, as he explained it to me, took place at the moment he understood the coming of omens, his inner power as it was juxtaposed against the world of nature. What he came to understand is that there are ways of being that are moved by the earth: sights and sounds one must be attentive to if one is to live in harmony. The faintest vibration, depending on one's proximity to it, can be the loudest scream. As he put it, "The recognition of omens comes out of the moment of turmoil—when you are right in that moment—as though the omens were there, but you do not see them until you are threatened."

Danger of the Darkened Clouds and Whitened Wings

Darkened Clouds find their way over
  the Darkened Mountains, over the

Darkened Soil, through the
Darkened Trees into my
Darkened Heart

There the clouds lay,
And for some strange reason
I want them to stay

Then deafening Darkened Thunder struck the Darkened
Tree I sat under,
the Thunder
Heartbeat of the Earth,
Made the tree fall, fall, fall and upon me and
there I lay
Under the Darkened Sky, beside
the Darkened Mountain, over the
Darkened Soil and with my
Darkened Heart under the Darkened Tree
A White Owl passed its wing over my
Darkened Eyes
the wing tempted me
Yet
I knew, I knew the Men in Skins
sent this prophecy to me in dream
Then I fell asleep with the tree on top of me

There in my dreams was silver sea
and turquoise trees
and fire burned in forbidden places
All was new, and man was but a granule of
sand in the blowing light purple wind

As the orange and yellow suns began to set
another man appeared on the surface of the Earth

Eagle on Mesa. Melanie Ellis (Oneida). I.A.I.A. Museum Collection.

Then I saw my dream more closely
  the man had a watch
  he looked to see
   time, time being contained and
As the orange and yellow suns set to rest
  before rest came about, they changed to red
   the man felt disharmony and was
    dismembered by a passing Wolf
I knew the sky would be red
   for all eternity

In the confusion I killed myself in a
dream, this dream it was
There I lay on the silvery wet sand
dead

I woke gasping for air, realizing that the tree
had rolled and begun to crush me
Alone I tried to move the tree
Then a passing man, a Painted Red Cheek
a brother of mine, raised the tree, and
in a twisting motion he was gone, gone into the
Earth, he died in my place, all that
was left was his night
cloak of Power

As I tried to rise, I found that my right leg was
broken, and a young Bear from
White Water carried me to
see his people in the
Mountains where
the snow was deep, they mended me and
taught me Bear Strength
And from an evil bow came
an Arrow Darkened by the Clouds of the Sky

It was meant for me, but, the son of White Water Bear people
took the arrow for me
he lay in my arms choking on his blood
a stream of his blood froze in the snow
the people of White Water Bear faded into the
whiteness, their future died in my arms
And I died a second time

As I walked through the forest the
      Creatures turned their faces
            from me to deny the act

"It wasn't my fault," I cried, but,
   nothing listened, except the Darkened Clouds
      I took my life for the third time...

(Time is not a dimension which I need to abide by,
      nor do I seek existence measured
            by time...)

Life was no longer a period of time
            Life became a small moment
There, I called to the Spirit to forgive me,
   All of the Earth and Sky watched to see
      my next action

Since I was taught Bear Strength, I sang
Bear songs for four days and four nights
this restored the White Water Bear and his people,
      their Power, and their Legend
The watch on the silvery wet sand had
      dissolved into the Earth

I woke.

The Darkened Clouds went back over the
      opposite side of the Mountains
And the White Owl lay in a dark part of the forest
      its back broken by my Grandfather

TOTEM POLE

◆ ◆ ◆

Cedar poles were carved by Turtle Islanders along the North Pacific coast from Vancouver Island to Alaska. They were of the following kinds: exterior and interior house poles, and memorial columns. Legend tells of the messenger from the sea, a medicine man who, during a drought, went to the beach to pray. He waited by the sea, and in time, a log pole covered with sacred carvings washed up on the beach. Soon afterward, the drought ended. The tribe then erected the pole in front of their village. This was how, in legendary terms, the exterior totem pole, celebrating the symbols of the tribe and its clans, came about. Anthropologists have pointed out that, for centuries, Koreans used wooden grave steles, markers or memorials. So it is certainly not farfetched to imagine one floating on the North Pacific currents, and thus finding its way to the northwestern shore of the United States.

Memorial or grave poles bore upon them the heraldic symbols owned by the family of the deceased. House poles, however, might be decorated with stories, some of which were sardonic or aimed at poking fun at certain other members of the tribe, or perhaps even outsiders. Only the wealthy could afford interior house poles, which stood in the middle of the house, directly behind the fire, marking the seat of honor.

To fully understand the Native American meaning of the totem pole, it is necessary to know, briefly, the nature of the northwest

Nimkish Village at Alert Bay.
Photograph by Edward S. Curtis.
Courtesy Rainbow Man, Santa Fe.

tribal person. Northwestern tribal culture was greatly concerned with two personal acquisitions: names and wealth. In a sense, this put it on equal terms with the culture at large. Further, the native appreciation of these two honorable ways of attaining status was not separate, but integrated. For instance, trading was common among the tribes and credit—another parallel line with general

American culture—was most important. It was an interesting custom of the Kwakiutl tribe that a man who did not have good credit could pawn his name for a year, during which time his name was not used.

And a man's name and his holdings—his position and his personal wealth—were very much entwined. The totem pole was a monument to both. However, the totem pole was not a monument to one man alone. A man's name was his fortune; so were the ancestors who bore that name, and the deities connected with them. All were part of the legend of his life, the accretions of honor, the events, recent and ancient, recorded on the totem pole.

The story is told of a Haida chief whose totem pole depicted the figures of Russian priests. The chief was proud that he had resisted the priests' attempts to convert him and his tribe. His record of resistance, recorded in wood, lived long after he and the priests were gone. The totem pole, therefore, served as family tree, family mythological reference, family symbol of wealth, and, in a way, a kind of tribal newspaper. Some students of Northwest tribal culture have compared the totem pole to the status and symbology of the automobile. And while one is stationary and the other mobile, both are concrete examples of personal and cultural identity.

TURKEY

◆ ◆ ◆

Once, long ago, the ancestors of today's Pueblo people gathered about them herds of long-legged, stalking birds. They herded them like cattle around the pueblo but treated them almost like pets.

Sacred turkey is most definitely not the bird of foolishness that is given seasonal credence, Thanksgiving and Christmas, by most white Americans. The people of Turtle Island treated the turkey as a bird of special virtue, a savior. Americans, too, it might be supposed, could do with a look at their own roots in this matter. For it was, in fact, the Thanksgiving turkey, that was given to the first settlers, the Puritans, by their Indian brothers and sisters during that first cold time of year, when the harvest was small and uncertain.

Native Americans honored Turkey Brother in all kinds of ways. Robes of glorious turkey feathers were worn by eastern and southern tribes. This was a bird of dignity and intelligence, not an easy bird to stalk and kill. (Once, perhaps more than twenty-five years ago, I chased a bunch of wild turkeys with a Navajo friend of mine in a lonely canyon in northern New Mexico. You could not sneak up on them and you could not keep up with them once they started off on a "turkey trot.")

During the great flood of the time when the Navajo people were

The Plaza at Walpi. Photograph by Edward S. Curtis. Courtesy Rainbow Man, Santa Fe.

just emerging from the depths of Mother Earth, Turkey proved to be their savior:

> As the waters rose
> The animal people
> Climbed into two reeds:
> Turkey was last
> To get into his reed—
> The foamy waters
> Whitened the tips
> Of his tailfeathers
> And they are white
> To this day . . .

Both Navajo and Pueblo people believe that Turkey carried in those same savior feathers the seeds from their former, primary world; so that when they came up into the next world, it was Turkey who seeded the fields for them. As ally, this is Turkey's role and power as a symbolic figure. Many tribes, it should be noted, did not eat turkey meat. The bird was kept around, if kept at all, as a pet, and as representative of the deity of legend, Turkey of the Seed-Gatherers.

Recently, I have heard it said by Native Americans that Turkey—and not Eagle—should be the guardian symbol of this country. Therefore, there is nothing so insulting, especially in the Southwest, where the old ways are still in practice, as the expression "You are a Turkey," or "What a Turkey that is," and so on.

Perhaps the expression ought to be "What an American you are!"—for, as one thinks about it, what could be worse than a person who, pretending to be grateful, uses one who has helped him, later switching his feeling of amity to enmity.

White Americans, ever hungry for what is not theirs, are like the dog with the bone. It was the people of Turtle Island who gave all that they had, so that when there was nothing left, they could then be told to go away.

The Arapaho Ghost Dance song says it well:

I liked the whites
I liked the whites

I gave them fruits
I gave them fruits

I am crying for thirst
I am crying for thirst

All is gone—
I have nothing to eat.

TURTLE

◆ ◆ ◆

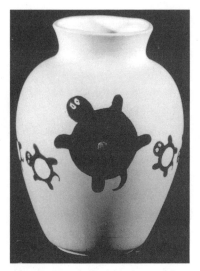

Above: Cast Ceramic Decorated Pot.
Buffy Dailey. I.A.I.A. Museum
Collection.

*Opposite: Sea Turtle Skull with
Shells.* Photograph by Bobbe
Besold.

The Seneca legend, common to many tribes but told differently by
each, describes a Star Woman who was banished by the Sky People
for uprooting a tree and making a hole in the sky. When she was
thrown through this hole by her own kind, the earth-surface creatures saw that she was going to fall to "earth." Turtle was asked to
dig down into the great water—for there was no land anywhere—
and find mud. This was packed onto her back to cushion the fall
of the Star Woman. Beaver was asked to pack the mud down. Thus
the birth of the Earth, Turtle Island, the Mother.

The connection between earth and sky is also seen in the
Cherokee turtle story that tells of the time of creation. This
version is from *Will West* by Paul Metcalf:

> Some hunters camping in the mountains . . . found two crea-
> tures round and large with fine grey fur and little heads like
> those of terrapins . . . on the seventh night they rose from the
> ground like balls of fire above the treetops climbing higher and
> higher until they were only bright points. The hunters then
> knew they were stars.

Native Americans celebrated the power of the turtle in various
ways. As a symbol of Mother Earth, certain southern and
midwestern tribes built great earthen turtle mounds, still visible

Sea Turtle. Monotype. Ross Lew Allen.

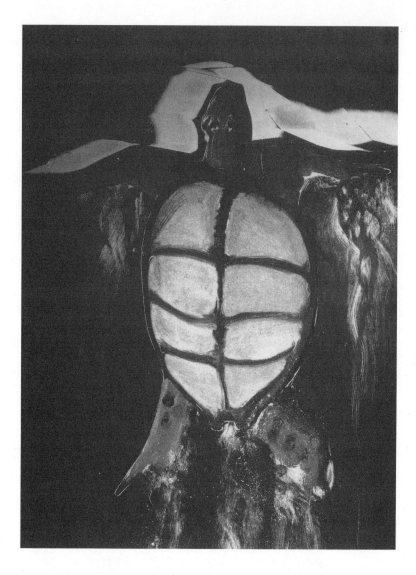

today. Turtle rattles and turtle shields are common throughout the tribes; turtle rattles are used today by the Taos Pueblo Indians (and other Pueblo people) during their Turtle Dance, a fertility ceremony heralding spring in the middle of winter.

The turtle, as symbol, is a creature of the three worlds of

creation. It lives in water but breathes air. It lives on land and water. Thus, the turtle tells of the joining of these worlds, a symbol of the fecundity of the mother. Unhurried and wise, she carries the world upon her back (a Buddhist/Hindu symbol as well as a Native American one). Changeless, the turtle, the wise old turtle, is the symbol of longevity and eternal life. As the primary symbol of the mother, the turtle expresses the belief that Indians have of Mother Earth's renewal. Countless times, I have heard the Native American opinion, injected into the ecology movement, that we must "let her alone and she will heal herself." And yet the "white argument" to this, always pragmatic, is, "How?" I have even heard Pueblo Indians say that they will not "recycle" because "the white man brought these things into the world, and he can take them out."

So, the turtle lives and cannot accept a meager "man-made" death.

The sea turtle's
heart
still
keeps
beat

long after you

thaw
the
meat.

Years ago, traveling on a busy road, I saw a great snapping turtle try to get across to the swamp side. There were impatient cars behind us and I knew one of them would kill the turtle, either on purpose or by accident, in their hurry to be elsewhere. So I stopped our car in the middle of the road, blocking traffic:

At the road's edge
between bridge and swamp
we watched the old hump-back
drag herself to the overhang.
I reached for the curved tail
too late: she struck the water
with a crash of spray,
drew herself in
and turned to stone.

U R N

♦ ♦ ♦

Native Americans have used urns to bury their dead, both cremated and noncremated, for hundreds of years. Stone urns have been
found in Southern California, the only place, perhaps, where stone
vessels were used. In other parts of Turtle Island, earthenware urns
have been discovered; also large seashells and the shells of turtles.
In Utah, burials of noncremated remains have been uncovered in
baskets. In northwestern Florida, urn burials consisted of a single
skull buried in the sand, over which an inverted bowl was placed.

Although some Indian grave sites were found by accident and
left as they were found, most have been plundered, and the
remains passed on to museums. Without question, this is a sacri-
lege and should not be permitted to continue. I once worked in an
office in Santa Fe where, during the remodeling of a bathroom, a
plumber uncovered the bones of an eighteen-year-old woman
who had been buried in the earth with her personal belongings—
bowls and other artifacts—for eight hundred years. Before the
owner of the building could forbid the disturbance of these
remains, they were illicitly carried away to a noted laboratory and
placed in a chemical-treatment bath. Later, they were taken apart
and codified for the dating process.

I was warned by a Pueblo friend at the time that this act, and its
subsequent reportage on television, would result in "something
bad" unless the bones and the belongings were returned and a

burial ceremony performed over them. With a friend I retrieved them and put them back in the earth where they belonged—but the damage had already been done.

The urn of time holds the pregnant mystery of the earth, but it is wrong to unearth it. Today, the culture at large seems to feel that discovery is more important than abiding mystery. Writer Linda Blandford has written in the *New York Times*:

> A few miles from Interstate 15, from Lawrence Welk Drive and Champagne Boulevard, from pink Italianate housing tracts on gray-scrub hillsides, the Pala Indian Reservation sleeps in another time, in the burning inland sun.
>
> Three thousand or so acres along dusty roads in northern San Diego County; a gravel pit rented out, an avocado farm managed by others, crumbling trailers slumped on or off brick supports and a soft thicket of willow trees, where the river once ran.
>
> In 1903, the Cupeno Indians were moved here by force from their homes in Warner Hot Springs. A photograph survives showing the morning of their exile: Stunned, proud, poor, they stand bundled in heavy Victorian clothing by neat adobe houses. Other photographs continue the story: the women saying goodbye to the graveyard, to simple wooden crosses marking parents, husbands, children. . . .

The author goes on to describe the graveyard today:

> . . . babies' graves and soldiers lost in service. The graves are covered with flowers, plastic, silk, fresh with ornaments and photographs, with stuffed toys, powder compacts, shoes and carvings—not one disturbed, nor one forgotten.

The grandson of the last survivor of the walk from home says, "Our people, they are nothing, but they are everything."

Left: Atsina Burial. Photograph by Edward S. Curtis. Courtesy Rainbow Man, Santa Fe.

This is a rare case where the people were moved and the graves were not. The burial urn of Native America is memory, living memory, because, as the late Charles Lovato of Santo Domingo Pueblo once said, without the past, there is no present:

Seasons without Spring.
Nights without stars.
Life without children.

It is time now to give back what has been wrongfully taken, to return the cairn to its rightful resting place. The urn of time, memory, cannot be "buried," but it must be put back where it belongs. It must be remembered. As the great-great-granddaughter of a survivor of Wounded Knee said, "It was a hundred years ago, and it seems like yesterday."

VIRGIN

· · ·

Nuestra Señora de Guadalupe.
Drawing and poem by Andrea
Bacigalupa. Courtesy Sunstone
Press.

Nuestra Señora de Guadalupe
Patroness of Mexico and All the Americas

Not to Montezuma or Cortes,
    Not in pyramid or colonial mission,
Not to prince of church or state;
    But the poorest of Indians, Juan Diego,
On a bleak, cold hilltop
Mary appeared.

She is roses in December,
    Water in the desert,
Serape against the cold,
    Sombrero for the sun,
    Guitar against the silence.

Maria, nuestra señora, mother to redman,
    brown and black and white,
Matrix of Americanos,
Madre de Dios.

The virgin patroness of the Americas is known as the Virgin of
Guadalupe. Her appearance on December 9, 1531, before a Nahuatl

man on a hill outside Mexico City marked the emergence of a Virgin Mary of Native American origin. The amalgam of Christian/Indian mythos here is quite striking; the Indian man who met the Virgin had been given the Christian name Juan Diego. He was standing on the ruins of the Temple of Tonantzin, the Mother Earth temple of the Aztecs, when she made her appearance as an apparition before him, announcing her patronage to Indian people.

Today she is revered throughout South and Central America as well as the American Southwest. Robert Boissiere speaks of his experience with the adoration of the Virgin of Guadalupe, who was introduced to him by his Taos Indian wife:

> I think the greatest of these pilgrimages to honor the Indian world patron saint was in 1954. That year the Pueblo of Taos brought the matachine dance team in which I myself participated. Santa Clara sent its buffalo and eagle dancers along with its governor. The success of the tradition we started was a miracle in itself, as remarked by Mrs. Clare Boothe Luce the year she deposited a plaque to commemorate the event. The plaque represented the Indian madonna which Mrs. Luce made in mosaic.
>
> Those incredible days will stay in my memory forever as the embodiment of faith in the Aztec maiden who promised succor to her race after the conquest of Mexico by Hernando Cortez.

I wonder whether the Virgin is, in fact, a blend of two religions—what might be termed old earth and new earth. Could the Madonna be a fusion of White Buffalo Woman (of the Sioux, Kiowa, and Cheyenne) and Mary, the mother of Jesus of Nazareth? White Buffalo Woman was an emissary of motherhood of Turtle Island. She voiced the word and power of the old earth, the turtle that would not change. The Virgin Mary, symbol of a new world, brought to the Indians by the Spanish, French, and English, was a figure of beauty and compassion. The two Madonnas, woven together like the weft of willow in a basket, have, perhaps, been threaded into a work of oneness: a belief of light and dark wood, two ways of seeing the same thing.

Driving across the mesquite barrens of Mexico, you will see the little roadside shrines of the Virgin of Guadalupe. She is virtually everywhere; from dawn to dusk you see her, framed and haloed in upturned, earth-implanted bathtubs and old discarded truck tires. Large and small, the Virgin sheds her kind glance across a burned and bitten landscape:

White Buffalo Woman said to the Oglala Sioux, "Tell your people that I am coming. A big teepee should be built for me in the center of the nation."

To Juan Diego, the Virgin of Guadalupe said:

Go and tell the Bishop of Mexico City that a temple should be built here for me so I can give all my love, my compassion, my help to my people. I am the merciful mother of all of you who live united in this land. . . .

WOLF

◆ ◆ ◆

In the book *Of Wolves and Men,* Barry Lopez tells the story of a Wolf Shaman of the Crow tribe. Here, in poetry form, is a re-creation of the essence of wolf power contained in that story:

Wolf. Monotype. Ross Lew Allen.

All this happened long ago
in Crow country.

One time a Crow warrior
took a bullet in the chest
that made a hole through him.

Three medicine men believed
he could be saved. One of
the men wore a wolf skin
and sang a wolf mother's
medicine song.

This medicine man
trotted and nosed the pup,
the wounded warrior. He
dipped his nose in water
and shook it on the warrior's
head, and he whined
like a wolf.

And she coaxed her pup to the river
where she bathed him and licked him
and cleaned his wounds
and returned him to life.

All this happened long ago
in Crow country
in Montana
in the land where the wolf spirit
is yet young
and strong.

The fate of the North American Indian and that of the wolf are deeply interwoven. The newly founded nation of America, in exercising its right to achieve "manifest destiny," had decided that anything that stood in the way of progress ought, on moral grounds, to be eliminated. The Plains Indian and the prairie wolf, by their very natures, expressed the natural longing for open territory in which to free-range. As "America" closed in on them, they fought back, were swallowed by the swell of the incoming tide, and eventually retreated. Today, they both live on "reservations."

Long ago, the Indian and the wolf sometimes hunted together. On the plains, tribesmen wore the mantle of the wolf, the cocked, pointed ears rising above the grassed headland of buffalo country. In the timberlands and the taiga meadows of the North, men and wolves hunted elk and caribou, not as competitors but as fellow huntsmen. Barry Lopez writes of this alliance, and of the hunting prowess the Indian got from the wolf, who was master of chase, face-off, and kill. The "dialogue of death," as Lopez calls it, involved the active and synchronized will of two animals: wolf and elk. In the stalk, the wolf sets out to track and kill its quarry, the elk. In the face-off, it is the locked eye of each that determines the outcome of the hunt. If the elk is not ready to be killed, then the wolf, during the ultimate confrontation, knows it. The fit, it would

My Eyes Looking Out at Wolf Now.
Monotype. Ross Lew Allen.

seem, recognized the fit. In gesture and stance, as well as the glance on the killing field, the killer will inquire of the quarry, "Are you ready to die?" If, through the face-off, the answer is "No," the wolf will surrender and move on.

In my own conversations with Pueblo bow hunter Larry Littlebird, he has remarked that the hunted, once stalked and ready for death, will either "surrender its breath" or it will refuse to do so, in which case, mystically, it is no longer the hunted. On the audio tape *Hunter's Heart,* Larry tells of two elk: one that does not give its breath, for its time was not yet come, and one that offers it to the hunter. The breath, according to Larry, is a palpable thing, an offering, a spirit presence in the air.

The lives of wolves, the stories told about them, and the history of the Native American people have similarities. Hunting in packs, they took meat back to their young. Both sang and danced in the good and bad weather, living close to one another. Loving the open range, for a time, they each had the freedom to come and go with the season. And, for a time (some say it is not yet over for either, though the implements of destruction get ever more sophisticated), each one—wolf and Indian—was trapped, hunted, poisoned, beaten, driven, riven, run down, clubbed, bagged, hanged, burned, skinned, scalped, and, finally, when there were too few to worry about, left to starve.

The Wolf In Us

The paw-print of a two year old Alaskan timber wolf,
  canis lupus pambasileus
   is the same size as the face
Of a three month old human child.
We humans fear the beast within the wolf
  because
We do not understand the beast within ourselves. What of
The nurturing mother wolf of Romulus and Remus fame?
Are the dreams of our mythic past, Little Red Riding
  Hood
And the Boy Who Cried Wolf, too much for us?
How many wolves have we murdered?
How many will we murder still before we can approach
  the animal
   look it in the face, and—not gouge out its eyes—
  but apologize?
What do we see in that sharpened snout with haunted
Eyes that makes us skulk in guilt, cowardice,
  shame and fear?
May we begin to look now?
May we see the truth? That the wolf in us is no longer
  afraid, and
Like the last flight of the swan will keep a long low
  to the water
   profile in the heart of humankind.

XAYMACA

$\bullet\ \bullet\ \bullet$

On October 12, 1492, Christopher Columbus landed on what is now known as Watling Island, one of the Bahamian chain. During this first exploration, he also traveled, as most of us know, to the north coasts of Hispaniola and Cuba. However, it was during his second voyage, two years later, that he arrived at the place of legend—"the land of blessed gold"—that he had been hearing about on the other islands. This was Xaymaca, or, as it is known today, Jamaica.

The name, probably of Arawak origin, has been translated as "the land of wood and water." And so it was: a place of such opulent greenery, with crystal freshets of water spilling from the earth, that, on May 5, 1494, Columbus wrote in his diary that he believed that he had discovered ". . . the fairest island that eyes have beheld." Paradise. And so it was that he claimed it for Spain, calling it St. Jago, Santiago, for that country's patron saint. During this visit, Columbus let the Arawaks know that he meant business. Thus he sent a number of crossbowmen onto the island to kill and subdue the peaceful natives. It was done. The following day, the people brought him gifts of cassava, fruit, and fish.

It was nine years later, on his fourth voyage, that Columbus made it back again to Jamaica. This time, he decided his two dilapidated caravels were not fit for the Atlantic crossing. In St. Ann's Bay, an arrow's flight from shore, the two vessels were sunk

Green Tree Frog. Monotype. Ross Lew Allen.

in shallow water. They still rest on the sandy bottom in the clear water of the bay at this writing, five hundred years later. For twelve months, Columbus stayed on the island of Jamaica, where he dealt with the combined adversities of hunger, hardship, and sickness. It wasn't until June 1504 that members of his crew made it to Hispaniola, returning to rescue the weary explorer and the rest of his stranded men. On June 29, Columbus and one hundred members of his party left the island for good. He would, in fact, never again return to the New World. However, his predecessors did, and they colonized Jamaica, setting up a southside city that, today, is known as Spanish Town.

What happened to the Arawaks, among the first Native Americans of the New World? They were enslaved and put to death. They were given the gift of disease, something that their immune systems could not hope to overcome. It did not take long for the Spanish, greedy to get on with the meaningful business of life, to finish them off. Soon they were gone altogether, and there was little enough to remember them by: some stone implements, a pottery vessel or two, a few words from their own language. Ironically, it was the latter that lived on into the twentieth century: *barbecue, hurricane, hammock, tobacco, canoe. . . .*

Recently, in the Parish of St. Mary on the north coast of Jamaica, not too far from St. Ann's Bay, one of the largest Arawak sites was located. I chanced to be living less than a mile from the dig and visited it on a daily basis. A wiry Rastaman watched over the place, which was located above the bush, overlooking the sea on a high promontory. It seemed that this particular group of Arawaks had picked one of the finest hideaways in all of Jamaica. The hillside was surrounded with large leaf trees, concealing the place. In addition, the dwelling, if such it can called, was actually a series of underground tunnels, naturally formed by an ancient pattern of reef fissures. All around the coffee-colored earth was scattered evidence of the people—ax heads and shards of pottery mostly.

I learned that the Arawaks had once been one hundred thousand strong. Living close to the coast and along the many fresh-water springs, they lived off the land, the sea, and the stream. Brown-skinned, short, slightly built, broad-faced and flat-nosed—so they were said to appear. In point of fact, the Arawak islanders of Jamaica had originally come from the South American mainland.

They liked to fish, grow tobacco and cotton. The latter took up much of the women's time: carding, spinning, and weaving. From the great Jamaican cedar and silk-cotton trees, the people made the hollow sea-worthy crafts known as canoes. In their spare time, they enjoyed playing a game that is widely popular today; in England, it is called football and in America, soccer. The Arawaks are credited with inventing the game.

Like their tribal counterparts in North America, the Arawaks believed that their ancestors came out of Mother Earth. They believed that after death, their souls migrated to a place where there were no hurricanes or droughts. In this place of no sickness, they lived forever. The place was called *Coyaba,* meaning "heaven." It was the same place that Columbus imagined he had sailed into on his first voyage to St. Ann's Bay.

The Market

      In the open-aired market
next to the ancient Anglican church
  with its door
Propped open
  by a goat's foot. By the cream-curdled shore of
The bay burned to a mirror finish in the sun, little
Sun chips flecking off into the blue distances
  to the final grey hairline of the horizon.

      In the mannish-water
Marketplace of olden time, the voices sing a song of
  sixpence: "Callaloo, callaloo, mango, mango."
The sun on the leaves is greener than money, brighter
  than fame
And the song floats up, butterflies melting, doctor-
Birds flitting: "Shrimp, shrimp, pumpkin, pumpkin."

      As we wander in and among
The hot stalls of paradise
Tipsy from the heat,
  rubbing shoulders
With the swarming lost balmy-smarmy bodies of this generous,
  mad, hopeful little long-gone starving island. Is it
Too late to call up Columbus with an obeah curse
  and make him
Into a whipping boy? Too late to recall the sick, sunk stinking
  ships
Of the Middle Passage, send them back to Africa and the
Cape of Good Hope? Too late to make it back to the Arawak
  meeting place of the soul, Coyaba
  paradise, pair-a-dice, seven, eleven, back in heaven?

YUCCA

• • •

Throughout the Southwest at elevations from three thousand to eight thousand feet, the bright candle blossoms of the banana yucca shine during the months of April, May, June, and July. Browsed by livestock, the pulpy fruit was to many Indian foragers an important item of diet. It was roasted and eaten immediately or dried and stored for the winter. Sometimes the fresh fruit was made into a fermented beverage. Out of the leaf fibers, sandals, baskets, and cloth were woven.

New Mexico's state flower, the so-called Spanish bayonet, is also known as the soapweed yucca. This narrow-leafed yucca comes in many shapes and sizes, from the low soapweeds of the upland to the treelike gorgons of the desert. The knife-sharp pointed ends were used by the early *penitentes,* the outlawed southwestern branch of the Catholic faith that still believes in self-flagellation to consecrate the flesh with wounds. The fruit of the soapweed yucca is not suitable for eating, but the Navajo have used the plant for centuries to make a classic kind of shampoo. They call it *yay-bi-tsa-si,* and it is unearthed, the root taken up and pounded with fresh water to make a fine sudsy foam. This is rubbed deep into the hair and scalp, and later rinsed off. The result is smooth, silken, shiny hair that stays that way for many days.

Yet another yucca, whose Latin name is *Yucca aborensis,* is described by Mary Austin in *The Land of Little Rain.*

Mescal Harvest. Photograph by
Edward S. Curtis. Courtesy
Rainbow Man, Santa Fe.

The yucca bristles with bayonet-pointed leaves, dull green,
growing shaggy with age, tipped with panicles of fetid, greenish
bloom. After death, which is slow, the ghostly hollow network
of its woody skeleton, with hardly power to rot, makes the
moonlight fearful. Before the yucca has come to flower, while
yet its bloom is a creamy cone-shaped bud of the size of a small
cabbage, full of sugary sap, the Indians twist it deftly out of its
fence of daggers and roast it for their own delectation.

The meaning and mood of the Southwest desert can be
witnessed in the yucca. The friars of the old missions called the
plant "our Lord's candlestick," for that is how it appeared to them,
burning in sun or moon, buried in its own daggery sconce, a
haven for small animals, lizards, snakes, feasted upon in the sappy,
sugar times by ants.

I have unraveled a piece of good strong yucca string from one of
the green sword blades, and made a knot of it. And I have ground
up the root in the Gila wilderness with a Navajo friend, and
worked the recalcitrant root into a suds bath for my hair. There
was a song my brother used to sing about the desert land, and I
always thought of it when, on a camping trip into the lowland, I

watched the moon rise from behind a fountain of yucca blossoms: "Beneath the yucca sand of the dry southwest land . . ." Here was fruit to eat and covering for the foot, a weapon, if one chose to use it as such, a giver of string, the yucca, a purveyor of baskets. The yucca is the symbol of survival, for in the most barren places, the most desolate moonscapes, it grows confident and strong, tough on the outside, soft in the fruity center. Like a man, the yucca does not reveal itself easily; you must get to know it; you must learn how to use it; you must approach it gently.

Washing Our Hair

To stoop into the water, head down and unpre-
  pared for attack,
Is one kind of trust.
Ah, yay-bi-tsa-si: dig you up out of the talus bed
Where you live, fat and sharp. Thing of
  the past, spiky poker, silk-stringed loafer
In the mean furnace of the sun, I dig you up,
  make a meager suds
Of your root, rubbing you on a rock, asking
  your permission
To make my hair clean and shine.
You and I, yucca yay-bi-tsa-si
Getting into the water
  merging with a humpbacked trout
  who has no flute.
Rub and soap, rub and soap—
  so little the desert offers can't be used,
  so little the desert has to be used,
Bless this plant I wear on my head,
  bless this head I've plaited with yucca soap
  Making us both
  yucca-clean.

ZIGZAG

◆ ◆ ◆

Zigzag is the Native American way, in English, to express the word for lightning. Lightning, the zigzag arrow of the deities, flung from high above in the sky, is a symbol of power and of danger. The Hero Twins of the Navajo were trained in the use of thunderbolts and thus were able to slay the evil giants that roamed the earth and whose blood one now sees in the desert, dried and magnificently contorted into the runnels of the ancient world.

Lightning, the guardian of cradle board and shield; thunder, the beat of the old drum. Lightning and thunder, friends who bring rain; enemies who turn capriciously and do dark things to earth-surface people. It is said, in Navajo stories, that shafts of lightning were once fired by children in the sky, children who were having fun—just like the children of the Navajo who shot arrows when they played at making war.

So the arrow at the beginning of this book is treated as an earthly representation of a heavenly thing. And lightning is that arrow personified into a being of incredible power. The thunderbird of legend carries the lightning bolt in her claws. In Navajo, zigzag lightning is *itsiniklizh*. It flashes four times, and, so the old ones say, always flashes back, upward, from where it comes. Zigzag: There where it strikes the ground, the old enemies of Dineh are cast into the ground. They say, "He hurls them into the ground with the lightning, one after another."

On the face of a warrior, the sign of the zigzag meant he would go and return, with vengeance. Like the lightning, he could not be touched, but that which he touched would be killed.

Not long ago, I found myself in the rather strange position of having to find the unfindable. I had been asked to locate a Navajo prayer for a friend of mine. The friend, a noted anthropologist, was conducting a funeral for her son's best friend, a young Iowa farmer who had been struck dead in his own field by a bolt of lightning. By accident—or blessing—I found the poem needed, freely given by my old Navajo pal Bluejay. Here, as it was written at the close of his visit, is that story.

Zigzag

He looked out the kitchen window in Tesuque. The sun was shining, the sky was a dancing summertime blue; the light breeze fiddling in the morning glories. Such a perfect morning to be alive. Yet, in the olden-time, Native American way, it was a good day to die.

The image of death affected Andrew as he sat and looked out the window. For it was on such a cloudless day, only the week before, that a close friend of his was running on the hill when, out of the dazzling blue, he'd been killed by a bolt of lightning.

How could it happen to anyone he knew? Such things happened in epic poems by heraldic poets. Not in real life. Not in the sand hills of New Mexico. But, yes, they did happen in the unaccountable desert, such things did happen. And when they did, they left people feeling hollow inside, buzzy and strange, and a little bit suicidal.

The call from Gloria didn't help much. "I've picked a statement to read at his funeral," she said. She showed him the dying words of Crowfoot, an orator of the Blackfoot Confederacy. In 1890, as the world of his people shadowed into twilight, Crowfoot spoke: "What is life? It is the flash of a firefly in the night. It is the breath of a buffalo in the winter time. It is the little shadow which runs across the grass and loses itself in the sunset."

Gloria, moments before Andrew went to the window, had alternately cried and laughed. The poem spoken by Crowfoot . . . the bright New Mexico morning . . . Gloria and the morning glories outside . . . their mutual friend, now dead. Out there in the incomparable southwestern sun lay the unspeakable jeweled morning. Andrew asked himself, again, how death could come sneaking up on such a fine, inexhaustible day?

Then a car rumbled up the driveway and a short, heavyset Navajo man got out, stretching. He walked to the door of the house. Andrew recognized Bluejay, his oldest and wisest friend on the reservation.

Old friend Bluejay.

After greeting each other with customary grins, Bluejay sat down near the kitchen table and accepted a cup of coffee. Then, as they started to talk, the phone rang.

Gloria.

Between apologies and tears, she said that she was having such a hard, hard morning. She just couldn't accept the loss. "I need something," she said, "and I don't know what it is." She wanted something that she didn't know where to find.

While speaking on the phone with Gloria, Andrew kept his eyes on Bluejay. Bluejay's face, normally immobile, was full of fanciful humor, like a cat casually playing with a piece of string.

Jay's father was a stargazer, a Navajo diagnostician, one of those rare, good men who knows how to consult the stars. A Navajo astrologer, but one who, unlike today's New Age breed, has not lost touch with the wisdom of honest starlight. A man who may, if he wishes, talk to stars; a man who hears them speak back in their own language.

Andrew wondered if Jay might have something to say to Gloria, for he was uncertain what to say himself. She was taking

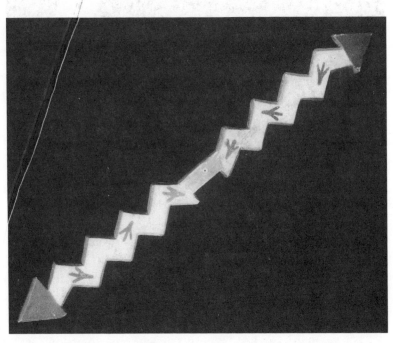

Pueblo Ceremonial Dance Wand, Lightning Stick Motif. Courtesy W.E. Channing & Co., Santa Fe.

this death so very hard. Thinking Bluejay might be able to console her, Andrew offered him the telephone.

He watched attentively as Bluejay cupped the phone to his ear, placing it against his shoulder. The playful light still on his face, he closed his eyelids, and listened.

Bluejay listened.

And listened.

It was an art, what he was doing—or not doing. His mind quiet, he seemed to meditate on each word that was said to him. His cat's face lost none of its bemusement, however, and the corners of his mouth turned up slightly, as if he were watching a mouse. His mustache quivered. Finally, after what seemed like an hour to Andrew, he delicately cradled the phone back into the receiver.

He was still smiling, inwardly.

Andrew said impatiently, "Well, did you help her any?"

Jay shook his head, eased himself into his chair. His coffee was cold now, but he waved aside Andrew's attempt to add warmth to it. The old familiar smile flickered across his face, stopping at his mouth, which was always kind of set in a smile. He did not really smile, but his face was so relaxed that he seemed to glow from within. The smile, if there at all, was an illusion. Something inside Bluejay was aglow, like a fire coal that warmed his belly without ever burning it.

"Life," he said philosophically, "is not separate from death. It only looks that way. So it is possible, sometimes, to laugh when someone dies."

Bluejay picked up the cold coffee cup, swirled it around a time or two, and put it back on the table.

Andrew nodded.

"Do you laugh when someone you love dies?" Andrew asked pointedly.

"That man who died," Bluejay said without expression, "is fortunate."

Bluejay's face, in repose, was quite ageless. His smooth dark-honey skin was shining. The reflection of well-being in his presence was so palpable that it did not seem possible that Bluejay would ever die. His face had the permanence of uncut stone.

Perhaps four or five minutes ticked by—an eternity, it seemed to Andrew.

Then Jay began again. "My father says: The corn grows so that it can make seed. The corn dies to make more corn."

Andrew felt like arguing.

"We are not corn, " he offered. "We're flesh and blood. There's the difference."

Bluejay smiled apologetically, as if he had forgotten to say something that would complete his thought.

"When you die," he whispered, "you return to Mother Earth. There's a song that goes something like this—

'Rattlesnake, the earth,
    lightning, the universe.
  When rattlesnake takes you, it is the earth.
  When lightning takes you, it is the universe.

    He is blessed, he is of the earth.
If he had lived, he would be like
    the lightning-struck tree
        that no one comes around.
Had he lived, no one would share
    food with him
        until he was blessed by ceremony.
Today, blessed by ceremony,
    he is of the earth.'"

Bluejay finished the song and sat in silence. The song had been a breath of life; now it was over, he was breathing a different song.

After a while he got out of the chair and went to the front door of the house. He did not say goodbye because he was not really leaving, just moving along.

Outside, in the noonday sun, he stretched. Andrew saw the playful light enter his eyes again.

"Now I must go to Albuquerque and mediate a Navajo-Hispanic dispute. It's my job. I'll sit and watch and wait. The big talkers will flex their muscles. Then they will ask me what I think about things. I won't say right away what I think. I'll let them think about what it is I am going to say and hope that they've at least heard some of what they themselves have been saying. The trouble today is that people don't listen anymore. They cannot hear themselves think or speak. They rush from one thing to another. I guess you could say it's just the American way. . . ."

"—And the Navajo way?" Andrew questioned.

Bluejay laughed, his whole face warming with pleasure.

"The Navajo way's to wait and watch," he said smoothly.

The two men stood by the door of Bluejay's Toyota Tercel. They seemed reluctant to part company.

Then Bluejay rolled on the balls of his feet and slid into the front seat. He dropped into it with a sigh.

Suddenly there was a long dry buzz in the air. Bluejay raised his eyebrows, leaned his head out the open car window. He looked uneasy.

"Did you hear that sound?" he asked his friend.

Andrew said, "Yes, a kind of rattling."

"Sounded like a rattlesnake," Bluejay said thoughtfully.

"No, I don't think so."

But even as the words escaped Andrew's lips, he wondered if it weren't so.

"Rattlesnake was telling me to shut up," Bluejay said seriously.

Then the old friendly, apologetic look came back into his eyes.

"—I guess not . . . If I'd said too much, I might've gotten bitten," he said, grinning.

The trill came again—a monotonous deadwood drilling kind of sound.

"Locust," Bluejay said. His face was relieved, the tension gone out of him.

Then he added, "That was a close one."

"Yes," Andrew agreed, thinking of something else, "a close one."

And for the rest of the day it looked like lightning.

BIBLIOGRAPHY

❖ ❖ ❖

Austin, Mary. *The Land of Little Rain.* Albuquerque: University of New Mexico Press, 1974.

Boissiere, Robert. *Po Pai Mo: The Search for White Buffalo Woman.* Santa Fe: Sunstone Press, 1983.

Bureau of Indian Affairs, *Blackfeet Crafts:* Washington, D.C.: Bureau of Indian Affairs 1945.

Bureau of American Ethnology, *Handbook of American Indians.* Bulletin 30, Parts one and two. Washington, D.C.: Bureau of American Ethnology, 1908.

Capps, Benjamin. *The Indians.* New York: Time-Life Books, 1973.

Craven, Margaret. *I Heard The Owl Call My Name.* New York: Doubleday, 1973.

Curtis, Natalie. *The Indians' Book: Songs and Legends of the American Indians.* New York: Dover, 1968.

de Groat, Jay. *Whimpering Chant.* Albuquerque: Pronto Press, 1980.

Edelman, Sandra A. *Summer People, Winter People: A Guide to Pueblos in the Santa Fe Area.* Santa Fe: Sunstone Press, 1974.

Hausman, Gerald. *Meditations with Animals: A Native American Bestiary.* Santa Fe: Bear & Co., 1986.

———. *Meditations with the Navajo: Prayer-songs and Stories of Healing and Harmony.* Santa Fe: Bear & Co., 1988.

———. *New Marlboro Stage.* Fresno: The Giligia Press, 1969.

———. *Runners.* Santa Fe: Sunstone Press, 1984.

———. *Sitting on the Blue-Eyed Bear: Navajo Myths and Legends.* Santa Fe: Sunstone Press, 1980.

Hoagland, Edward. *Walking the Dead Diamond River.* New York: Random House, 1974.

Holling, C. Holling. *The Book of Indians.* New York: Platt and Munk, 1935.

Hunt, Ben W. *The Golden Book of Indian Crafts and Lore.* New York: Simon and Schuster, 1954.

———. *Indiancraft.* The Bruce Publishing Co., 1942.

Hutchens, Alma R. *Indian Herbology of North America.* Merco, 1969.

Insight Guides. *Jamaica.* New York: Prentice-Hall, 1984.

Kloss, Phillips. *The Great Kiva: A Poetic Critique of Religion.* Santa Fe: Sunstone Press, 1980.

———. *Rainbow Obsidian.* Santa Fe: Sunstone Press, 1985.

La Farge, Oliver. *A Pictorial History of the American Indian.* New York: Crown, 1956.

Larrick, Nancy. *Room for Me and a Mountain Lion.* New York: M. Evans, 1974.

Levitas, Gloria, Frank R. Vivelo and Jacqueline J. Vivelo. *American Indian Prose and Poetry.* New York: Capricorn, 1979.

Littlebird, Larry. *Hunter's Heart.* Santa Fe: Lotus Press Audio, 1991.

Lopez, Barry Holstun. *Desert Notes.* New York: Avon Books, 1976.

———. *Of Wolves and Men.* New York: Scribners, 1978.

Lovato, Charles. *Life Under the Sun.* Santa Fe: Sunstone Press, 1982.

Metcalf, Paul. *Patagoni.* Penland: The Jargon Society, 1971.

———. *Will West.* Asheville: Jonathan Williams, 1956.

———. *Apalache.* Berkeley: Turtle Island Foundation, 1976.

Michener, James. *Caribbean.* New York: Random House, 1989.

Mooney, James. *The Ghost Dance Religion and the Sioux Outbreak of 1890.* Chicago: The University of Chicago Press, 1965.

National Geographic Society, *The World of the American Indian.* Washington, D.C.: National Geographic Society, 1974.

Stoutenburgh, John Jr. *Dictionary of the American Indian.* New York: Philosophical Library, 1955.

Waters, Frank. *Masked Gods: Navajo and Pueblo Ceremonialism.* New York: Ballantine Books, 1973.